#MTPCON 25

PRODUCT-LED SALES

Combining the best of Product-Led Growth and Sales

VINCENT JONG

ISBN Ebook: 978-84-09-59803-8

ISBN Paperback: 978-84-09-59802-1

If you have any questions about the content in this book, you can ask them for free at the link below and I will get back to you personally.

Thanks, and I hope you enjoy!
Vincent

www.PLGandSales.com/hotline

CONTENTS

RETAINING AND GROWING EXISTING CONTRACTS

THREE STEPS TO GET STARTED

ONWARDS

When PLG meets Sales

The big idea of this book

You've heard about Product-Led Growth (PLG). You know it's a Go-to-Market strategy that uses the software you sell to drive growth. You've read how companies like Slack and Zoom have used PLG to grow explosively.

But if you've grown your business through traditional sales, you might be wondering if PLG can do anything for you. You might be wondering:

- What are the fundamentals of Product-Led-Growth?
- Can I combine PLG with my sales team?
- Does it mean I have to lower my prices?
- Is it going to cannibalize my existing revenue?
- Does it mean I have to transform my entire company?

Here's the missing piece of information: ***you don't have to choose between PLG and sales.*** It's not one or the other. There's a middle ground.

That's the big idea of this book: you can combine the power of PLG with the value of a human touch in sales. The combined strategy is Product-Led Sales (PLS).

The earliest definition of PLS was something like this:

> ***Use a product-led approach to onboard customers, for example via a free trial, and then use a sales team to reach out to customers who demonstrated qualifying behavior.***

But in this book, PLS means:

ANY combination of a product-led approach and a sales team.

The reason is that there are many more ways to combine PLG with sales. You could for example have an outbound sales team call customers and invite them to sign up for a free trial. We'll discuss the different options in the subsequent chapters.

My obsession with PLS started with a firsthand learning experience. I was brought in as a product leader at Dealfront, which was the result of a merger between two businesses. My mission was to make sure the solutions we offered could work and grow together. I soon realized we were in a unique situation.

One company (Echobot) had been growing through a traditional sales approach. The other (Leadfeeder) had been leveraging Product-Led Growth supported by a sales team. Both companies had built these models out at scale. At the time of the merger they were similar in employee count and revenue but in other ways, they couldn't have been more different.

1. Echobot's model focused on maximizing the initial contract value with the customer. Even if this resulted in a longer sales cycle. This is common in a traditional sales strategy. Leadfeeder operated a high-velocity model. The goal was to close an initial contract as fast as possible and grow the contract later.

2. For Leadfeeder, product metrics were a key part of the Go-to-Market strategy. They were always talking about "product-qualified leads". These were people who had made sufficient use of the product to justify the sales team getting in touch. For Echobot, the product could only be accessed after signing a contract. Thus, product metrics were not of interest during the sales cycle.

3. These two strategies also translated into the organizational structure. Leadfeeder had more product related functions in place, like Growth, Product Marketing, and Product Analytics. Echobot didn't have any of these teams. However, they did have people focused on Sales Enablement and Account Management, which Leadfeeder didn't have.

Our goal was to get the best of both worlds. So we cross-pollinated the Go-to-Market models and we started to learn how they could benefit from each other's approaches. We were combining a product-led approach with a traditional sales model, with both models fully deployed and revenue in double-digit millions on both sides. It sounded like an exciting challenge when I joined and it didn't disappoint.

This book explains everything I learned from this experience, as well as my 8 years as founder and CEO of a PLG-driven business called FunnelFox. My perspective is unusual, because I've seen this problem from every angle.

As a founder, my focus is on how to build a successful business; as a product leader, my focus is on the customer experience and how the product can drive growth; and having been a sales rep early on in my career, I also know what it's like to be at the forefront of the business.

However, one person can never know it all, so I wanted to include other points of view on Product-Led Sales in this book. Each chapter includes a related interview with a leading operator or thought leader. They will share their experiences with Product-Led Sales at companies like Amplitude, Snyk, and Leadfeeder.

This book will help you combine PLG and sales in the way that's right for your business. You'll know when a product-led approach makes sense, and when it's best to use sales. You'll be able to find the best of both worlds and unlock growth that wouldn't be possible with just one approach; all without losing the momentum and customers you have today.

4 Core PLG principles

If we want to combine PLG with sales effectively, we need a common understanding of how product-led thinking differs from traditional sales thinking. Similar to the definition of PLS, I use a broad definition for PLG in this book:

PRODUCT-LED GROWTH

Any Go-to-Market strategy in which the (software) product a company sells drives growth. For example, it may drive customer acquisition, user onboarding, or contract expansion.

Now let's talk about the 4 core principles of PLG:

1. Product-Centric
2. Self-Service
3. Value First
4. Data Driven

I'll discuss these, each in turn.

Product Centric

The first principle of PLG is *focus on the role the product can play in the Go-to-Market*. PLG doesn't rely on customer-facing teams. Instead, a product-led approach uses the features and capabilities of the product to drive growth. The product can guide users through different stages of the customer journey or it can provide the sales team with better leads based on customer behavior in the product.

PLG and sales have different approaches to releasing new features. Leadfeeder used phased roll-outs: a new feature would first be made available to a sub-set of customers in a soft release. Later, there would be a launch to the wider public — only after the product metrics looked good. At Echobot, the sales and

Customer Success (CS) team started selling the feature as soon as a first version became available. In their case the selling process provided the product feedback required to mature the feature.

I have even worked at companies where we'd start selling a product before it was even built. In traditional sales, you can do that. This wouldn't work in PLG, because the product itself needs to do the selling. This means you will only know if it's going to sell once the product experience has been released.

Self-Service

The second PLG principle is *offer a self-serve experience.* Implementing PLG doesn't mean that the entire customer journey needs to be self-serve, just some of it. To have the product guide the customer on their journey, the experience needs to be intuitive.

At Leadfeeder, the entire customer journey was available through the product, from onboarding to paying, and there was a segment of customers who never spoke with anybody in the company. They tried the product, learned how to use it, and bought it by themselves. Echobot followed a more traditional model. Potential customers were offered a product demo by the sales team. They would then be onboarded by CS to make sure they knew how to get value out of the product.

The Leadfeeder user was guided by the product, while the Echobot user was guided by the CS team. Leadfeeder also had a Growth role, which specifically focused on conversion steps in the product. There was no such role at Echobot.

As one of our early considerations, we needed to decide which parts of the combined platform we wanted to make compatible with self-service and make sure that the product-led principles would be applied there.

We agreed we wanted to have product-led onboarding available for all our products. We looked at this area first because onboarding is one of the most fundamental parts of any product-led strategy. Also, as we combined our products into one platform, we wanted our customers to have a consistent experience.

The idea of product-led onboarding is that a user can get started with the product by themselves. Onboarding is almost always a good investment as it helps customers get value from your product. The primary outcome of product-led onboarding is higher adoption of key features. This in turn leads to better sales, customer satisfaction and retention. For this, the product needs to be intuitive to use so customers can find their own way around.

At Echobot, we had some products that required onboarding training, so we explored how we could make the onboarding for these products more intuitive. This did not mean we were going to introduce a free trial from the outset (this is a separate consideration, which I'll cover later). We first needed our customers to be able to onboard themselves after signing a contract with sales.

Value First

The third core principle of PLG is *deliver value before trying to sell anything*. In practice, this often translates into driving usage. We assume that more product usage will lead to more value delivered. Therefore we expect a higher chance of making a sale. Common examples of this approach include a free trial or a free version of your product. Leadfeeder offered both of these options.

The entire approach of Leadfeeder's Go-to-Market was aimed at getting the customer to use the product. Active usage was the most reliable indicator that someone would buy. Echobot showcased the unique data capabilities of the solution in a sales demo but to work with the data themselves, a customer would need to sign a contract first.

In some cases, Echobot did offer trials or share data samples but it was an option for the sales team to use if a customer had doubts. With Leadfeeder, using the product was always part of the path to buying it: value first, sale second.

Data Driven

The last PLG principle is *be data-driven.* Specifically, product data drives decisions. Key product experiences, such as user onboarding, need to be managed and improved continuously. This requires the same attention to detail as a marketing funnel. Even the text or color on a button can influence results. This means you need to have detailed tracking and always work to improve these metrics.

Of course, both companies were collecting data on product usage. Though as with the previous principles, there was a difference in how these metrics were used within the company. For Leadfeeder, product metrics (e.g. usage data) were core business KPIs. They were always part of the Go-to-Market conversations. For Echobot that wasn't the case, nor did Echobot have a Product Analytics department. This work was done by Customer Success and Product Managers.

This understanding was essential when discussing the possibilities of PLG for the combined company. It helped us identify where we needed to change our approach. Both companies had product event tracking in place, so we just needed to tie the metrics to business impact.

We started by aligning the definitions of activation and

engagement because these stages existed both in the product-led and the traditional sales process. Activation would tell us how well the onboarding was working. Usage data would tell us if customers kept using the product. A decrease in usage was an early indicator of churn. We made these metrics part of the Go-to-Market conversation. This helped us understand how valuable our products were for customers.

Next, we looked at how these product metrics could help us predict customer behavior. We then empowered the CS and Account Management teams with this information. We created Disengaged reports, highlighting significant deviation in product usage per customer. We sent Slack messages to the teams if things suddenly changed and we analyzed product behavior to assess whether some of our other products could be a good fit for a customer.

As we mastered these foundational product metrics for Echobot's products, we could start thinking about other product-led approaches. At this point, we still leveraged our customer-facing teams for the interaction but product data helped them decide which customers to focus on.

Interview with Pekka Koskinen

Leadfeeder, Dealfront

Secrets to success from Leadfeeder's growth model

"We knew that if somebody takes a trial, then we can demo the product with their website visitors, with their customers. It's way more powerful."

- PEKKA KOSKINEN

About Pekka Koskinen

Pekka is the co-founder and former CEO of Leadfeeder. He also successfully built and exited 3 other businesses. These include a software development company called Solinor and a payment gateway company called Payment Highway. In 2004, he founded Snoobi, a web analytics business which provided much of the early learnings for Leadfeeder. The earlier businesses have all been sold and today he is fully focused on Dealfront - the result of merging Leadfeeder with Echobot after a €180M investment from Great Hill Partners.

Main takeaways

- With outbound sales they saw best results when they guided customers to the free trial and only tried to close them after they had seen their own data.
- Leadfeeder hired salespeople who could help customers get value from the product and prioritized this over traditional sales skills.

- Their preference for PLG was based on lessons learned from running Snoobi, where they struggled to scale internationally with an outbound sales approach.
- They constantly monitored conversion rates and the effectiveness of sales to identify the most promising segments to engage the sales team on.
- Leadfeeder developed their approach since 2012, long before terms like Product-Led Growth and Product-Led Sales were a thing.

The full interview is available as a write-up, podcast, and video.
www.PLGandSales.com/interviews

Key considerations for PLG

Why PLG matters today

Echobot hadn't applied PLG to its products before the merger but the team had been exploring possible applications. That's not surprising. At the time, PLG was a big topic in the B2B software community. Many companies were considering whether this was a direction they should follow.

Part of the motivation came from the very public success of some of the early adopters of PLG. Having seen companies like Dropbox and Zoom skyrocket, everybody wanted to do PLG. This was in part because the product-led strategies applied by these companies had a much wider reach than traditional approaches. As a result, success stories were very public.

A company selling $20k contracts through traditional sales needs only 500 customers to make $10M in annual revenue. A product-led company selling user licenses at $20 per month will need 40,000 paying users for the same revenue. So this kind of product-led approach tends to reach a much wider audience.

Besides this, other trends in the B2B software market have been driving interest in PLG.

Increased competition

The emergence of cloud computing has dramatically decreased the costs of starting a software company. New companies can now get the hardware they need on demand, from cloud providers such as Amazon Web Services. This eliminates the need for heavy upfront investments.

In the sales and marketing space where Dealfront operates, this has led to a true explosion of software vendors. The annual

MartechMap from www.chiefmartec.com illustrates this well. The map covers companies in marketing software. The number of companies grew from 150 in 2011 to 11,038 in 2023. And all these companies are trying to reach the same small group of decision makers at our target customer.

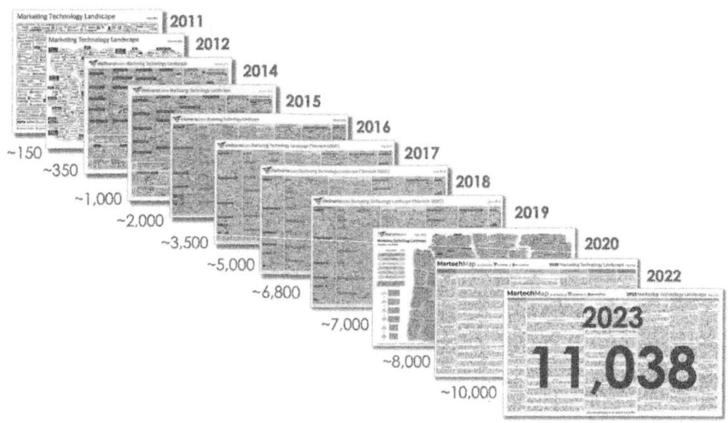

Evolution of the number of companies on the MartechMap

This is one example, but similar developments have happened in other software categories. It's only expected to become easier to set up a company. Today no-code solutions allow even non-technical people to build an application and improved AI assistants can answer technical questions, make suggestions for implementation, or even write the code for you.

With this level of competition, making it easy for your customers to learn about your solution is key. This is where PLG comes in. It allows your customers to try your software before they buy and it can enable you to reach the users of your software first, before getting to the buyer.

Evolved customer buying behavior

Newer generations of buyers have taken decision making positions. This has changed the behavior of customers when it comes to buying decisions. Before a potential customer is ready to speak with you as a vendor, they will already have done their homework.

This includes online research into the topic. They will ask their network for recommendations and read reviews online. The sales rep is no longer considered a reliable advisor in this process because they have an obvious bias toward the solution they sell. And because customers now have all these other options, they no longer need to rely on this biased view.

With PLG, a company can engage a customer in the earlier stages of the buying journey. Customers may not be ready to buy, but they might be willing to try your solution. For many customers, the best way to know if a solution will do what they are looking for is to try it out.

This is exactly what a product-led approach can enable. The buyer retains their independence in the buying process. They get to interact with the company and the product to make an informed decision about whether they want to engage further.

Financial pressure

The global recession in 2022 caused a lot of Venture Capital (VC) funding to dry up. This funding previously drove the growth of many software companies. Suddenly, VC investors started to talk about profitability and efficient growth instead of the growth-at-all-cost approach they had been advocating previously.

This came at a time where many existing sales models were

already under pressure and seeing a significant decrease in effectiveness. Increased competition and automated sales rep outreach had flooded decision makers' inboxes and it has become very hard for sales and marketing teams to cut through the noise.

The drive for efficient growth made companies reduce the investment in their sales organization. Many are now looking at PLG as a way to improve their sales strategy.

Different ways to leverage PLG

When a company considers adopting PLG in combination with a sales team, there are many ways for PLG to add value. These approaches can be divided into three main categories. Each has its own dedicated chapter in this book.

1. Reaching new customers in your market
These applications of PLG introduce your brand or product to new potential customers. For example, you can gain new customers through the product experience (Acquisition). Also, you can get customers to promote your brand to a wider audience (Marketing).

2. Engaging and converting your current audience
This focuses on companies that are already considering your solution. For example, they may have visited your website. Applying PLG here can mean converting them from an anonymous website visitor to an engaged user (Onboarding). It can also mean converting onboarded users to paying customers (Qualification and Conversion).

3. Retaining and growing existing contracts

You can also apply PLG to your existing customer base. This can have a meaningful impact on the results of the company. This category focuses on customer engagement and contract renewals (Retention) and finding opportunities to grow a customer's contract size (Expansion).

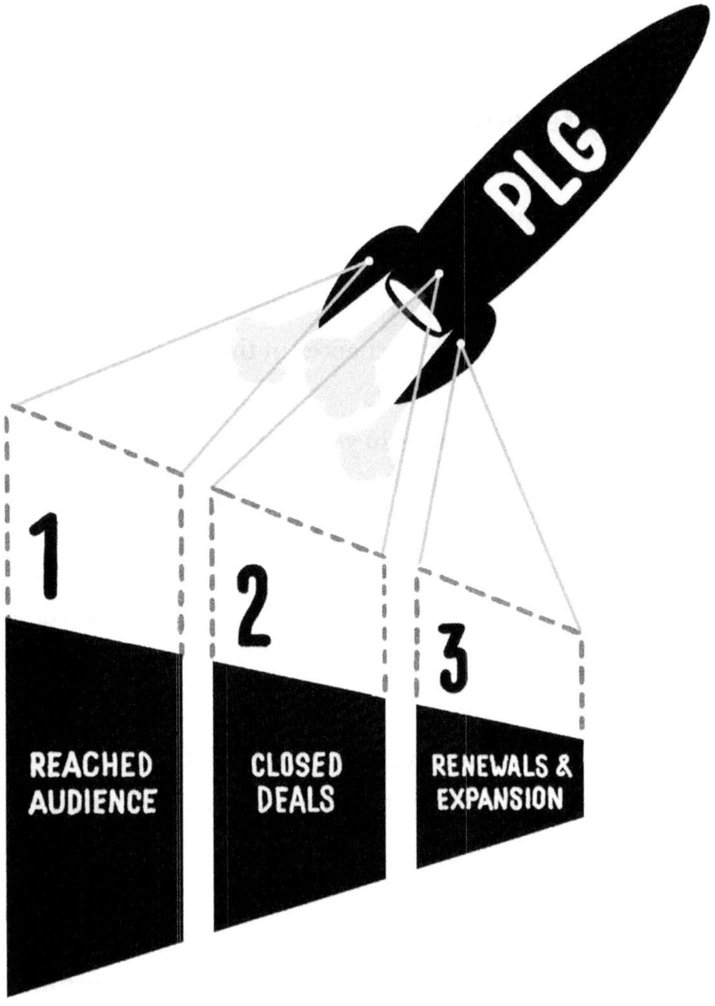

A key consideration for any company looking into PLG, is which customer segment will get the desired results. A company with a large customer base might first look at expanding existing contracts. This is typically lower effort and lower risk. Another company might focus on a more efficient sales approach to give their company faster or less expensive growth.

When you start applying some elements of PLG, you don't need to become a fully product-led company right away, if at all. You can transition gradually and build confidence in the product-led philosophy. At every step, you can decide whether it is still the right direction for the business.

PLG is not fast or cheap

One common misconception I'd like to debunk at this point is that PLG is fast or cheap. It can be cost-effective because it scales well, but getting to results requires time and resources.

The success of a product-led experience is influenced by a complex set of factors. These include messaging, the user experience, and timing. It's unrealistic to think you will get these all right on the first go. It takes many iterations before they all perform well.

In a traditional sales approach, a sales rep can quickly respond to what they are hearing in the conversation. If they learn that the prospect is looking for something else or doesn't have the budget, they can adapt. They can then present an offer that fits these circumstances.

In the product you typically don't have this flexibility. The experience, messaging, and model have been designed with a certain customer journey in mind. Customers who don't fit within that journey may not feel addressed by the value proposition.

Applying changes to a product often takes time. It requires design and implementation before you can do anything. Getting PLG right requires continuous work and usually means a substantial investment of resources.

Getting the first customers through a PLG approach is thus neither fast nor cheap. The real benefits come only when the approach starts to work. PLG scales much more efficiently than a traditional sales approach. Growing it from 10 to 1,000 customers can be much more cost effective.

Common pricing models

PLG is closely tied with the Software as a Service model, so the pricing models follow a similar pattern. Let's go through the most common pricing models and their implications. Keep in mind that many companies combine multiple models in their pricing and packaging.

Seat-based subscription

We'll start with one of the most well-known examples which is seat-based pricing, in which you set a price per user. As new users get added, the total price for a given customer increases. You multiply the number of users by the unit price to get the total price. This is a common model for sales technology, such as CRM systems, and productivity or collaboration tools.

This kind of pricing can facilitate a bottom-up customer acquisition model. Single users within a company decide to use the product by themselves and can pay for it with their own credit card. That often works for seats up to $100 per month.

As more users are added, this creates enough momentum for the company to buy the solution for the broader organization.

Generally, this model fits well within PLG. Product-led motions can draw new users into the product. These new users can then become customers themselves or be added to the existing company's invoice. A challenge of this model is that every new user becomes a budget consideration for the customer.

Our Sales Intelligence solution at Dealfront includes seat-based pricing. The number of users that get access to our company and contact dataset, defines to a large extent the pricing for a customer. This is because every user can identify new companies they want to sell to. They can also find the right people to speak with and figure out how to reach out to them. As this is the primary value of this solution, it makes sense to have seat-based pricing.

Usage-based pricing

Another model in PLG which is becoming more common is usage-based pricing. Instead of paying a monthly subscription fee, a customer pays for what they use. This brings more variability to the revenue a company receives. It gives the buyer more control, while at the same time scaling better for the seller. The more value a customer gets, the more they will be paying.

Modern usage-based models often come with a freemium model. This includes an allocation of free usage, often by month. Freemium allows customers to test the software without having to pay. If the product delivers, usage will go up and they will enter the paid usage tiers.

When entering a paid usage tier, there are two main options:

1. **Pay As You Go**, where usage is counted throughout a month and the total is billed at the end of the month. This gives customers complete flexibility on how they want to use the solution. A good example of a company applying this model is Amazon Web Services. They track usage of cloud infrastructure throughout the month and bill at the end of it.
2. **Tier-based usage**, where usage is classified into predefined tiers. Each tier is often treated as a form of commitment. This gives the seller more certainty around recurring revenue, even if the customer's usage drops in a subsequent month.

These tiers can also protect the customer from expected fluctuations in the usage. Our Web Visitor Identification solution at Dealfront is priced based on the number of companies we identify on your website. The monthly volume of website visitors can vary throughout the year and identified companies can fluctuate significantly.

Were we to apply a Pay As You Go model, a customer's bill would fluctuate in the same way. Instead, we take the 12-month average of the traffic to smooth out the variations. Then, we define the usage tier based on this figure. Even if customers exceed their tier during their contract, they will not face sudden changes in pricing.

Different customers will prefer different models. It's important to listen to your customers when deciding which option to go for.

Data Monetization

There is one more monetization model worth highlighting in the context of PLG, which is data monetization. Consumer applications such as Facebook or Google often use this approach. They offer products that may be used free of charge. They then exploit the user's data to generate revenue, for example from advertisers.

This model also exists in the B2B space and in a similar way often comes with a free version of a product. Some solutions you can use for free but any data that goes into that product becomes part of the provider's dataset that they sell to others.

A common example is selling aggregated, anonymized data as benchmark data. Most customers don't object to this kind of information being used by a company as long as it's anonymized and unrelated to their company.

In the Sales Intelligence space, some of the biggest players in the category offer free versions of their products that pull contact details from your email account or CRM. Then, they sell this data to their other customers. The approach is laid out in the Terms and Conditions but companies I have spoken with were mostly unaware and unpleased that this was happening.

At Dealfront, we have decided to avoid such practices. We have ethical objections to them, as well as concerns around legal compliance. This is a consideration each company needs to make for themselves. Data monetization can be a source of brand and legal risk but if the practice adds enough value, you may decide that it's a worthwhile strategy.

I encourage you to be mindful of your customer though. Operating ethically, transparently, and in compliance with the law is important and recommended if you want to build a sustainable business.

The Land and Expand strategy

With PLG, the experience tends to focus on the specific use case a customer is interested in. The goal is to convert a customer as quickly as possible on that use-case and only once they've become a customer, do we introduce further offerings. This is known as a Land and Expand approach.

An important enabler of this kind of approach is the associated pricing model. For example, if you don't have extra seats, credits, or modules to sell, then a Land and Expand approach will not be a natural approach. That's because there's nothing to upsell. Let's explore some of the pricing considerations for a Land and Expand approach.

LAND AND EXPAND STRATEGY

The "Land and Expand" strategy focuses on getting an initial foothold within a company as quickly as possible. Then, it expands the contract value from there. It prioritizes velocity to close the first deal over maximizing the value of that deal.

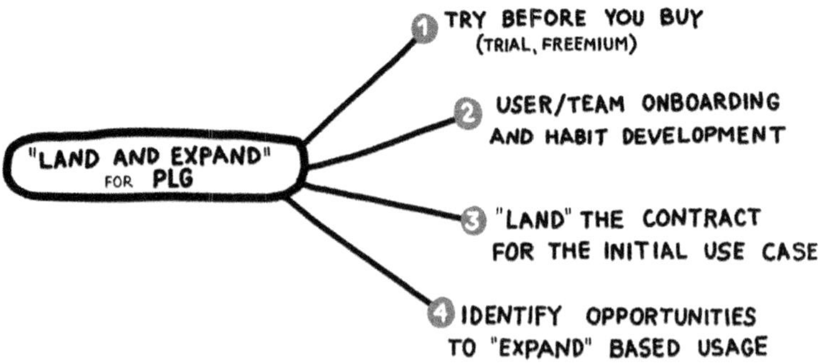

Pricing transparency

Pricing transparency is common in PLG. It means publishing the pricing structure on the website or making it easy to find once a customer engages with your product. This is quite different from traditional sales, in which pricing is often hidden behind a "Contact Sales" button. Some companies never share the pricing model at all. They present a customized offer to every customer once the needs have been understood through conversation.

In the early days of PLG, only companies with subscriptions below $100 per month had transparent pricing. Today, companies like HubSpot and Totango also openly share their higher priced plans, even if these are priced at several thousand dollars per month.

Customers have grown tired of traditional sales practices and don't want to jump through hoops to get the pricing. Many companies have now broken this mold and no longer require this secrecy. They just share the pricing on their website. Looking at my own buyer behavior, if a company does not state the price on their website, I assume they are more expensive than other options in that space. So unless they are a leader in their category, I will explore other options first.

Transparency requires a more thorough definition of your pricing model and removes some flexibility. In traditional sales, if your pricing doesn't match a customer's needs, you can fix it by giving a discount. In PLG this is harder because there might not be a conversation at all.

If your pricing is not transparent, you can change it overnight. With transparent pricing, this is harder because the pricing is likely visible in the product. Product changes might be required to update the pricing. In addition, pricing is on the website and a price decrease may encourage existing customers to switch to the new pricing. This could lead to a drop in contracted revenue. So you will want to have run some experiments before making larger changes.

Enabling expansion

In addition to the question of transparency, consider the structure of your pricing. In PLG, pricing is often designed to enable expansion within a contract, based on usage or the number of seats. This approach to pricing is also common in a traditional sales approach. Yet, it's applied differently in a product-led approach.

A traditional sales approach may require a customer to commit to a usage volume in advance. For example, they might have to commit to "up to 100 users." By contrast, a product-led approach is typically more dynamic. It can keep track of the number of users and charge based on actual usage. This follows the product-led principle of providing value before charging the customer.

Slack is a good example of this. They will automatically adjust the bill based on the number of active users in Slack during a month. They don't charge for the 100 users who might have created an account at any point in time. They charge for the 30 who are actually receiving value and are using the solution.

HubSpot is a good example of a company with pricing that lets customers grow within their plan. The company offers different plans with access to different features. Within each plan, they look at the number of contacts a customer has in the HubSpot CRM. They also consider the number of users that have access to their tools. Both these elements impact the final price. So a small startup and a large enterprise company could be on the same plan but pay very different amounts.

One more pricing element is important in PLG. It's how your company manages adding and removing user seats in your model. If every new seat requires another invoice, this creates friction in the buying process. Companies such as Figma have made it incredibly easy for any user to invite new people to their team on Figma. They will only charge for these users when the next invoice comes up. Before that invoice is sent, the customer receives a reminder to check if these new users should be added. If they disagree, they won't be charged. This allows users to start using Figma and learn how it adds value in their day-to-day. Otherwise, they may never have purchased a license.

Should you change your pricing?

While the ideas above may sound appealing, publishing your prices may also backfire. It depends on what you are selling, to whom you are selling, and what your competition is up to. Changes like this will impact revenue directly, so this will need to be tested properly before committing.

If your company has strong brand value, you might be able to avoid publishing your pricing. Customers will generally still want to speak with the best player in the market, even if there is a bit more friction in the buying process. Equally, if none of your competitors show their pricing, then there might be less pressure for you to do so. Although it's likely a matter of time until someone does so and unlocks a customer segment with it. The market trend seems to be moving more towards transparency, with the exception of high-value enterprise contracts.

Generally, I think any company will benefit from exploring how they can expand a customer's contract. This kind of growth would be based on the usage or size of a customer. Most software companies already have usage or seat-based pricing. Making it easy for customers to access and expand their contracts is a no-brainer and can be a good product-led approach to start with.

Interview with Kyle Poyar

Openview, Growth Unhinged

Overcoming pricing challenges in the transition to PLG

"Focusing on enterprise customers doesn't mean the same thing as not doing Product-Led Growth."

- KYLE POYAR

About Kyle Poyar

Kyle is an Operating Partner at OpenView, an expansion stage venture capital firm. He helps their portfolio companies fuel growth and become market leaders. Before this role he spent almost six years at Simon-Kucher & Partners consulting top technology companies on their packaging and pricing and Go-to-Market strategy. He is also known for his weekly newsletter Growth Unhinged, in which he covers in-depth case studies and deep dives on product-led growth (PLG), pricing, and Go-to-Market strategy.

Main takeaways

- Many companies fear cannibalization and giving away too much in a freemium. These fears often become the reason the PLG strategy fails.
- Usage-based models tend to be a good fit for companies who are doing sales today when introducing PLG. They can be combined with the existing pricing more easily.
- According to the SaaS Benchmark Survey, companies

vary in their PLG adoption. This variation depends on industry, target customer size, and software category.

- PLG can enhance efficiency and lower customer acquisition costs. This is a necessity in markets where high-touch sales are not economically viable.
- Kyle warns against undermining PLG efforts when transitioning to enterprise-focused strategies. This risks losing the large pool of users necessary for sustained growth.

The full interview is available as a write-up, podcast, and video.
www.PLGandSales.com/interviews

How one plus one becomes three

Sales Assist: Guiding instead of selling

When you decide to implement PLG, that doesn't mean that you will no longer need a sales team. There are many ways in which sales and PLG can be combined. The most common combination is for the sales rep to contact users who have reached a certain point in the self-serve journey. This role is called the "Sales Assist" role.

A Sales Assist rep will only contact a customer after they have completed certain steps of the onboarding process. That's a different customer profile than the typical lead in traditional sales and this has implications for the way you can talk with these customers.

Selling to self-serve customers

When a user signs up for your product, they trust you enough to share their email address so they can try the product. It is important to realize that this person is not at the same stage of the buying journey as an inbound lead. Someone who requests a demo expects to have a call with a sales rep. A person who signs up expects to get more familiar with the product without necessarily speaking to anyone.

A large and growing segment of customers want to do their own research before they talk with somebody. Since the rise of the internet, customers have been much more empowered to do their own research. PLG enables the next step of this trend. It allows customers to explore the product on their terms and make sure it meets their requirements.

This changes the role of the sales person. If you start a sales pitch to a customer who's in a self-serve experience, you have a good chance of scaring them off. These new users are getting to know your product. The best thing you can do is to offer them guidance and help them get to value. Even if they don't all engage, that's OK, because the product is already guiding their engagement with the company. This is why many people who are in a Sales Assist role have a title like "onboarding specialist" or "success coach".

Focus of the Sales Assist team

Sales Assist comes into action when a new user becomes a Product Qualified Lead (PQL). At this point, they should have received enough value from the product to be open to a conversation.

Each company can define PQLs differently. This is highly specific to your product and process. For example, for Leadfeeder, a PQL is someone who has integrated the tracking script on their website. A scheduling solution like Calendly might require action from multiple users because the revenue from a single user is much lower. The company needs an indication that a larger contract can be sold before they engage their sales team.

PRODUCT QUALIFIED LEAD:

A Product-Qualified Lead is a company that has received first value from the product. This is independent of firmographics, such as employee size or industry, and demographics, such as geography or job title. Please note that a PQL refers to the company, not the user. In the same way, MQLs and SQLs in traditional sales refer to the company to which you are trying to sell.

MQL, SQL & PQL		
	WHAT IT MEANS	EXAMPLE DEFINITIONS
MQL	A good-fit lead.	Did qualified marketing actions like booking a demo and/or fits the Ideal Customer Profile.
SQL	A lead with purchase intent.	When a sales rep creates an opportunity or after a good first call with an Account Executive.
PQL	A lead that has received value from the product.	When a lead completes certain setup steps, is seeing first results, or is collaborating with team members.

Once Sales Assist gets in touch, the conversation focuses on helping the customer progress on their journey. This could mean helping the customer to configure the product. You might show them how value is created, explain common use cases, or help them onboard further team members. Later in the journey, it may also mean helping the customer navigate their own organization to gain budget approval or helping them secure payment of the invoice.

In some cases, Sales Assist reps can also make better offers than the default offer in the product. Some Sales Assist reps can even deactivate the self-serve buying functionality for a customer to deliver a consistent buying experience when a different offer has been made.

No matter the tactics used, the main goal in all interactions is to help the customer progress. This is a different experience from traditional sales.

Balancing between self-serve and Sales Assist

The Sales Assist team increases conversion rates in the product-led buying experience. Before PLG became mainstream, this was referred to as "sales assisted conversion". For example, in 2019, Tomasz Tunguz touched on assisted conversion as part of the Redpoint Free Trial Survey.

600 companies had submitted their data for the survey. They found that for companies with a free trial and self-serve conversion, the median conversion of a lead to a paying customer was 4%. For companies where a sales person was involved in the free trial process, the median conversion rate to a paying customer was 15%. That's almost a 4x increase in conversion rate due to Sales Assist.

While this is a steep increase, it doesn't mean that every company should implement Sales Assist. Its effectiveness depends on the volume of customers, the self-serve conversion rates, and pricing. It also depends on how the engagement of Sales Assist impacts the conversion rate.

To illustrate with a simple example, if you sell a product at $10/month per user, calling every single user will be too expensive. However if you sell a $300/month solution, it may actually pay off if you see similar results as in the mentioned survey.

Segmenting for value potential

Customer segmentation can also play an important role in the Sales Assist decision. It may generate a good return on investment for some segments, but not for others. A common example of this is when companies set a user threshold at account level in their PQL definition. This is often applied when the price per user is low, such as in the $10/month example mentioned before.

The company then looks at the number of users to assess if a customer is engaged enough to qualify for a larger contract.

This is common with bottom-up models, in which any user can start using the product on their own initiative. Activation of one user is not enough to engage the Sales Assist team. This could be an individual who is giving the product a try without having the intent to buy a larger contract.

Companies with this type of model want to make sure that there is a certain commitment from the customer before Sales Assist engages. Otherwise the conversion metrics will not support the investment in a sales team.

You might also combine user behavior with (parts of) your Ideal Customer Profile and only trigger the Sales Assist team to reach out to companies that match this definition. A simple example of this is to segment by geography and only reach out to customers in core geographies or in areas where your sales team speaks the local language.

Sometimes companies will decide to always reach out to certain segments, regardless of the behavior in the product. This can make sense with high value customer segments, where even a low conversion rate can still pay off.

At my previous company, FunnelFox, a PQL was a company that connected their email and CRM account and invited at least 2 colleagues. However, whenever a company with more than 1000 employees signed up, we knew that they would typically not be able to connect their CRM due to permission restrictions. So we would reach out soon after the initial signup. Even if only a few converted, those contracts were higher value and the approach was still profitable.

It's worth highlighting that with Sales Assist, even if the customer doesn't engage with the sales rep, the self-serve experience will still allow them to buy. The Sales Assist interaction is optional. It's only if the customer agrees to engage, but it's not a requirement for buying, as it would be in traditional sales. So of those users that don't respond to your sales team, some of them will still become a customer.

Driving the right behavior

The goal of Sales Assist is to make sure the customer gets as much value as possible out of the initial experience. This may mean that the Sales Assist rep helps with the customer's initial onboarding to set up their account. This is especially true if the setup is too complex for people to complete by themselves.

The team could also share best practices on how to engage with the product. For example, how to get the right notifications or integrations set up to ensure the product integrates well into the customer's day-to-day. They might also help onboard the rest of the team, if this is important for customer value and converting to paid.

These examples show that the Sales Assist role helps the customer use the product. It drives metrics such as activation, engagement, and adoption. The aim, as with unassisted PLG, is to enable a high velocity sale and not to confuse the customer with other offers.

The right time to reach out

The next question is what will trigger Sales Assist to engage with the customer? At FunnelFox, we focused Sales Assist on customers who had connected their CRM and email.

Connecting these accounts was the first step people needed to follow when setting up their account. At the same time, it is a relatively big step that requires trust. By this stage we know the customer has reached a certain level of commitment in trying out our solution. It also meant we are now processing live data for this customer, so we could show value when engaging in a conversation.

We investigated whether reaching out earlier was worthwhile to help people get set up. However the conversion rates on assisting prior steps were too low. These segments involved a mixed bag of both committed users and people who were not convinced. So, when you pick your trigger event, it's important to look at the conversion rate of that step in the customer journey and assess the increase you can achieve.

There are two things you can do if the conversion rate you are seeing is not high enough to justify the added cost of having a team in place. First, choose a moment further down the customer journey. Hopefully, you will have filtered out more of the uncommitted customers by then. Second, improve the product experience leading up to the newly defined trigger. This will maximize the number of people that make it to this point.

Compensation for Sales Assist

In PLG you want to convert a user to a paying customer as fast as possible. This is different from a traditional sales approach where the aim is more often to maximize value on the first transaction. Commissions provided to traditional sales reps incentivize this behavior. They don't usually reward later contract expansion.

In the past years, I've seen more companies updating their sales compensation plans by adding rewards for expansion within the first year after closing the deal. This shows that even in traditional sales, there is a trend towards prioritizing speed over initial contract value. This is a much more customer centric way of selling; one with less risk of overselling.

Avoiding overselling is a must, especially in a product-led approach. You don't want the pursuit for maximum value to prevent you from closing a deal in the first place. Therefore even while other teams may be involved in closing the expansion, part of the commission for that goes to the sales rep who brought in the deal.

To prevent sales reps from focusing on maximum contract value, you can also actively manage the length of the sales cycle. This includes both the time it takes and the number of calls. With Sales Assist, there is typically a set process. There are few touchpoints and a specific number of weeks for expected results. Sales reps who regularly exceed the average are unlikely to prioritize speed. This makes it a good indicator for investigation.

For Sales Assist reps specifically, there is another dimension to compensation. That's to define which leads are counted towards their commission and if that includes assigned leads who don't engage and buy through self-serve. What's important to keep in mind is that incentives drive behavior, so any metric you use needs to drive business value.

My preferred approach is to count all assigned customers towards commission. I want the system or person that does the assignment (i.e. lead routing) to decide if the customer counts. This removes the need for any further definition. It also encourages the sales rep to treat all assigned leads equally and it allows the company to update the assignment logic over time. For example, they could decide not to assign certain segments to sales reps anymore if that's not profitable. They could also decide not to assign segments that convert by themselves in self-serve. It's the cleanest and clearest way I know of.

An example of a less ideal metric for assigning commission would be if the sales rep has emailed the customer. Since this requires no engagement from the customer, it won't be an indication of any impact.

Some companies only offer a fixed salary to Sales Assist reps. This benefits the company because it ensures that each customer gets fair attention. It also emphasizes a focus on onboarding, rather than selling.

My personal preference though is to have commission included. It helps drive important business metrics that are hard to influence elsewhere. For example, you can give a significantly higher commission for annual plans than for monthly plans. Both are available in the self-serve interface but a sales rep can influence that decision. Commission can be a valuable tool in driving such outcomes.

Sales Assist is a catalyst

As with everything in your Go-to-Market approach, you'll need to keep looking at how the numbers develop over time. Sales Assist is a catalyst for the product-led journey, however, it does not replace the product journey. One of our experiences during the Dealfront merger serves as a good reminder of this.

In the first year of the merger, we brought the Echobot and Leadfeeder products together under the new Dealfront brand. Many people were still finding us through the websites of the original companies but if you started a trial on the Leadfeeder website, this would create a Dealfront account. Even though the onboarding experience was the same as before, our conversion rates tanked.

While we were still getting the same leads in and had the same Sales Assist team in place to speak with customers, the brand change was too sudden. This spooked users and even with a sales team in place to contact them, we were no longer able to convert them. Conversion rates recovered once we started to show "Leadfeeder by Dealfront" instead of only Dealfront: a small change with a disproportionate impact.

I see this as a testament to the unique state of mind of a user who signs up for a free trial. If the product doesn't meet expectations or is confusing, then there is not even enough trust to take a call with an onboarding specialist.

Calculating the return on Sales Assist

When you deploy sales assist in your customer journey, make sure to look at the metrics per customer segment. Different regions and customer segments might respond differently to the Sales Assist role.

You'll want to keep an eye on the Return on Investment (ROI). If you have the conversion rate of the self-serve experience, calculating the ROI for Sales Assist is straightforward. You take the additional number of deals, multiply this by the Annual Contract Value (ACV), then compare that with the cost of the required sales reps and the expected revenue increase they should bring in.

Let's go through this with a worked example:

- Let's say your self-serve conversion rate from signup to paying customer is 5% and with Sales Assist you are converting 15%. If self-serve closes 10 deals per month, then that becomes 30 with Sales Assist. Meaning 20 more deals per month or 240 per year.

- If your ACV for these customers is $3k. That means you are making 240 x $3k = $720k in additional revenue per year due to Sales Assist.
- Now let's say a Sales Assist rep can close 5 deals per month. That means you'll need 4 people to close those 20 deals. For easy calculation let's say those reps cost $100k per year. So in total the cost for the Sales Assist team is $400k.
- Then we compare the $720k increase in revenue with the $400k cost. In this scenario a Sales Assist rep is returning 1.8x their cost.

Traditional sales companies often aim for a return of at least 4 to 6 times the cost of a sales rep. When deploying Sales Assist, a return of around 2 times the cost is not uncommon. Small changes to this formula can also make a big difference. For example, if your ACV is $6.5k instead of $3k, then you are doing close to 4x OTE. And if a Sales Assist rep can close 10 deals per month, then you only need 2 reps and with that you are close to 4x OTE again.

You can control these variables through pricing, productivity, and customer segmentation. As with any Go-to-Market model, experiment with different settings of these variables. Fine-tune the machine until it gives the optimal result for your business.

Sales-Led combinations

Sales Assist is currently the most discussed form of Product-Led Sales. Sales Assist is a common first place to look for companies that have a product-led approach. They are looking to close more deals from that self-serve audience. However, companies can combine PLG and sales in many other ways.

For companies growing through traditional sales, a good starting point for PLG can be Go-to-Market efficiency. Product-led experiences can help provide the sales team with better qualified leads. This can improve their closing rates. It may also improve the economics of an existing approach or it can enable you to serve an audience that currently would not be profitable.

Go-to-Market efficiency

The Customer Acquisition Cost is rising in most industries. Many companies need to revisit the economics of their Go-to-Market model. PLG can bring back efficiency and can open up new market segments or enable a company to have a financially viable sales team in the first place.

To understand this, we first have to debunk a misconception. In the B2B software market, many believe it's not profitable to run a sales team for annual contracts below $10k. In a purely traditional sales approach, this would require extremely high performance but that rule of thumb doesn't apply if you support this same sales approach with PLG.

There are a few calculations that lead people to the $10k ACV rule of thumb. The easiest one is to look at the number of deals a sales rep needs to engage on. Let's take a $5k ACV and assume a sales rep makes $100k annually. If we apply 4x OTE then they need to return at least $400k in revenue.

That means 80 deals per year or 7 per month. If you do well and close 20% of the customers you engage with, that means 35 new deals per month. This is not impossible but if you have multiple steps in the buying process, this becomes challenging. Especially as the engagements compound month over month.

Yet if the expected closing rate of an engagement goes up to 40%, then this changes the picture completely. Managing 18 deals per month is much more manageable and can be scaled across a larger team.

With regular demo requests or outbound leads you could not achieve such a high closing rate. But with product-qualified leads, who have already understood the value they can get, this becomes a possibility.

The same goes for Customer Success. Most companies will not assign a CSM below a certain revenue threshold to maintain a profitable operation. Yet with the right support from the product and a lighter touch approach from the CSM, this also can be made more efficient. Providing this level of customer service can set your company apart from competitors and become a differentiator.

With PLG, the previous cost constraints are no longer relevant. You can even support the selling of $3k annual contracts with a sales team, as long as you leverage the product to qualify the customers who will then convert at the high rates you'll need them to.

So you can use PLG to make your existing sales approach more efficient and support Go-to-Market models and market segments that were previously considered unprofitable.

Product-Led, Sales-Led, or something else?

Something that in my view has caused some confusion in the market is the term "Led" in Product-Led Growth. When PLG was introduced as a term, it focused on the top of the funnel. It described an approach of acquiring new customers through viral functionality. For example, existing users can invite new users or users can promote your brand to their network. In those cases, the Go-to-Market is truly "Product-Led" as the product is the first step of the journey.

The scope of PLG today also includes companies that offer a free trial on their website. These companies may not deploy the previously mentioned tactics. They may drive people to their website through SEO articles that the content team writes or through paid advertisements. Then, they use the product to onboard customers. This is no longer truly "Product-Led". The first step comes from marketing, which would make it "Marketing-Led".

I've found that labeling approaches as being "Led" by something is not very helpful. It makes finding effective growth models for a company more difficult. I have intentionally chosen to avoid the term "Sales-Led" throughout this book. Instead, I refer to traditional sales. Sales can come at the beginning of the customer journey, like with outbound, but, it can also come later in the journey, like with any form of inbound.

I prefer to look at this as a set of growth tools. You have marketing, sales, product, and further approaches such as partnerships and communities. You can use them in any order in your Go-to-Market, as long as the approach drives results. Don't limit your creativity by thinking you have to lead with one tactic or the other.

You'll have noticed I still decided to call the book Product-Led Sales, because that's the term that people think about when combining PLG with Sales. PLG has become synonymous for any customer journey driven by the product. Similarly, Product-Led Sales has become any combination of PLG and Sales a company can deploy.

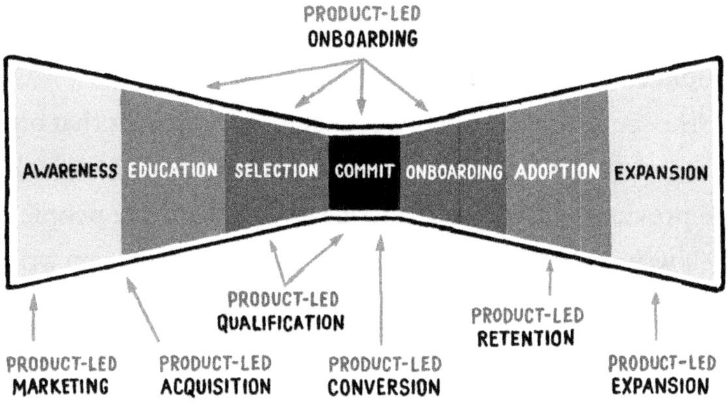

Different ways PLG can influence the steps of growth for a B2B SaaS company.

Based on the Bowtie model by Winning by Design

Requirements to combine PLG and Sales

You may wonder at this point if there are any requirements or rules for combining PLG and sales. There are some practices that seem to work for most companies, such as the ones I've covered in this chapter, but there really aren't any rules in terms of how the two can be combined.

What might not have worked for many other companies might work just fine for yours. It all depends on whether it fits your target audience and product positioning. Most markets are competitive these days, so doing things that competitors aren't doing could give you a competitive edge. Especially providing a human touch, where your competitors cannot.

I sometimes hear an objection that PLG can only be applied to low value contracts. For example, single user licenses or contracts that don't exceed a few hundred dollars per month. Indeed PLG can work well for those contracts but it can also acquire potential customers for a $100k contract.

It's true that customers who spend $100k on a contract often want to speak with a person before signing and that the buying committee is more complex than selling to a single user and their personal credit card. But this doesn't mean you cannot use PLG as part of your Go-to-Market. Especially if you want to use it to make your sales team more effective or improve retention.

Think of the qualification of customers who are ready to expand their contract so you don't need to chase customers on a quarterly basis. The product can identify exactly which customers are ready to buy at any point in time. This will ensure that sales reps spend their time on leads with a higher likelihood of closing.

PLG can also help by communicating the value the product has delivered for the customer. Larger buying decisions are made by multiple people and not all of them may be daily users of the product. So creating awareness of the value of the product can improve closing rates and drive better retention.

While a higher contract value can provide further requirements, there's no universal rule around contract value that decides if PLG can be a good fit. The only real rule to keep in mind is that you need to experiment with many different things and look at the data to decide what works best.

What to measure

To assess the impact of PLG in your sales approach, we need to understand which metrics matter. These metrics can also be used for internal communication. It helps align an organization around a new product-led approach, especially if all they know today is traditional sales. In this section I will cover the most foundational metrics.

Product metrics in a B2B context

Before getting into the actual metrics, one thing is important to call out in the context of B2B. A considerable amount of PLG efforts focuses on the user experience but we need to remember that, as a B2B company, we are selling to a business. That means we should not only look at the metrics at user level but also look at the metrics at company level (sometimes referred to as "team").

Of course the company level metrics are an aggregation of the user level metrics, so if you are getting started, you'll first need to make sure that the single user experience is successful. Once that's the case it's important to evolve past this, because team or company metrics typically drive conversion to paid customers.

User acquisition metrics

The first group of metrics to get familiar with involve the acquisition of new users. This starts with source attribution or in other words, knowing through which channel an account was created.

Attribution can be challenging in B2B. Multiple individuals from a company may interact with your company through different channels. If you have no experience with B2B attribution, start by tracking the last channel a user came through before they signed up. This is referred to as "last-touch" attribution.

There are more advanced ways of attribution tracking, such as Marketing Mix Modeling. I won't cover those here as B2B attribution deserves its own book. Just keep in mind that while last-touch is simple to apply, you might not be seeing the full picture.

When defining the different sources against which to attribute, don't stay at the highest level. If you only measure "paid ads" or "product" as source attribution, your insights will be shallow. To understand what works, you need to know which paid ad campaigns or product experiences drive results. Results will likely vary wildly between different sub groups.

When looking at channel conversion, look beyond user and company numbers. Also, bring in the revenue you're generating. A particular source may have a lower conversion rate. Yet, it brings in higher value customers.

To summarize the basics of user acquisition metrics:

- Map your acquisition channels – in as granular a level as possible
- Measure the traffic each channel creates and how it converts to new users and companies
- Remember to measure total revenue and revenue per customer for each acquisition channel

If you are using growth tactics such as user invites or branded content sharing, you'll want to measure those well. This can be done by calculating a viral coefficient, for which you multiply the number of referrals per account with the conversion rate of those referrals. For example, if an account brings 4 referrals on average and 30% of them convert, your viral coefficient would be 1.2. Any value above 1 means that this approach is accelerating your growth.

Activation metrics

Once people start using your product, your next focus should be on activation metrics. Different companies define activation in different ways. I define activation as the steps from account creation to the habit moment. Account creation will typically equate to the first user that signs up for that company. The habit moment is when the company is repeatedly gaining value from the product. It's the first sign of a habit.

There are three parts to measure in activation:

- **Setup** — Was the account successfully configured? Is the customer able to generate the intended value from the product? If a new user for a scheduling solution does not connect their calendar, then setup has failed. Setup can also include inviting other team members if that's required to get value from the product.
- **First value** — Also called the "aha moment". This is the first time your customer perceives the potential value of your solution. They might not get all the value just yet, but they are starting to see how you will get them to where they want to be.

- **Habit moment** — The moment at which you see first signs of a habit. Depending on your product, this might be on 2nd time use (for example checking weekly reports). In other cases, you may want to see daily usage for a week, before calling it a first sign of habit.

With activation, the importance of tracking metrics at the company/team level becomes clear. The first user who signs up may not be able to complete all the activation steps. They may need to invite another user to handle this. So, if you only measure this at the user level, you will miss important information.

A good example is the activation within our Leadfeeder product. A key step in this process is to integrate the Leadfeeder tracking script on the company website. Some users don't have access to the website so they need to invite another user to take care of this step. That means we need to track this activation step at the account level to understand the progress. Furthermore, the configuration is often done by marketing, whereas identified companies on the website are picked up by the sales reps on a daily basis. Once again, we need to look at the usage across the company account to measure if we are delivering repeat value.

In the customer journey, activation steps are typically measured only once. This creates different customer segments:

1. Those that didn't get set up.
2. Those that got set up and got first value but didn't repeat.
3. Those that started to actively use the product.

Engagement metrics

As an account gets to their habit moment, it will end up in the third category which is often referred to as "engaged". At this point the focus moves away from onboarding to monetization and retention. The goal is to keep the customer in this engaged state where they receive value continuously.

It's key to identify when usage drops for a company. When that happens, the received value starts to go down. This is a strong predictor of churn and identifying this early gives the company a chance to prevent it. Accounts that drop out of the engaged state can be categorized as "At risk" or "Disengaged".

Most companies set a lower limit of the minimum usage per day/week/month to be categorized as engaged. That still leaves a wide variety of engagement states beyond that definition. The usage for a 5 people team will look very different from a 100 people team. Even though they might both meet the minimum engagement level.

Therefore I found it best to look at variation in usage per account. When a customer's usage changes meaningfully, it means something is changing within that company. So the account may require extra attention to prevent becoming a churn risk. Usage variation tends to be more relevant than a general definition of good usage.

In B2B, it can also be helpful to track the engagement of specific key stakeholders. Think for example of your internal champion. If that person stops using the solution, that can be an important signal. It could even mean that they have left their position. In which case you'd need to make sure you remain well-positioned with the person who's taking over.

To summarize, the following metrics are most important

for engagement. Typically these are measured over the last days/weeks/months:

- State — Engaged or At Risk/Disengaged, based on company definition of engagement
- Engaged Users / Teams — Users or Teams that met the requirements for engagement.
- Engagement Variance — Any deviation in usage from mean usage in the previous periods.
- Specific tracking for key stakeholders within the account.

At Dealfront we measure Engagement Variance using a Z-score function. We create a weighted value from some of the key usage metrics, like the number of active users, value events, and sessions. We then compare these values to the mean we've been seeing for this account. A deviation of more than a few percent is a reason to investigate the account.

New business metrics

Besides product usage metrics, we need to track revenue metrics like new business revenue. These metrics are largely the same as with traditional sales in B2B, so I will only highlight a few.

We will want to keep track of the Average Revenue Per Account (ARPA) of new customers. The ARPA together with the conversion to paid, provides the business with important information. Think of the value of the currently open pipeline and the budget that can be spent to acquire new customers.

Product Qualified Leads are also an important PLG specific metric related to new business. This metric needs to be part of new business conversations, if you want to become more product-led.

To summarize the key metrics for new business:

- Average Revenue per Account (ARPA)
- Conversion to Paid — Per customer segment and channel
- Product Qualified Leads (PQLs)

Retention and expansion metrics

Beyond new business there is of course retention and expansion. We have already covered usage retention under the engagement metrics, so here retention refers to contract renewal.

Again the definitions here are the same as you'd use in any B2B software business but given the importance of these metrics, I wanted to include them nonetheless:

- Customer Satisfaction — Satisfaction measurements can be a good indicator for churn. Think for example of the Net Promoter Score. These are especially powerful when combined with engagement metrics.
- Churn — Customer churn is a lagging indicator of an unhappy or underserved customer. Even though lagging, it's important to track as it directly impacts revenue.
- Expansion — Any contract expansion revenue generated. For example by increasing the existing usage or adding new products to the contract.
- Net Revenue Retention (NRR) — NRR assesses if the total revenue from a certain group of customers increases or decreases over time.

As we'll see in further chapters, retention and expansion are a key part of many product-led strategies. Tracking these metrics accurately is therefore an important ingredient for success.

Comparing Go-to-Market models

When introducing PLG, you need to be able to decide if the new approach is better than the original model. For a fair comparison, don't just look at the number of closed deals but compare the total output of both models.

Defining what success looks like

PLG has many applications, so it's important to define success before adding product-led elements to your Go-to-Market. This definition will depend heavily on the PLG strategy you've chosen to implement.

For example, you could be leveraging product-led principles for customer acquisition. This may require you to invest significantly to make your product's onboarding more intuitive and get a good ratio of users who invite others. So you'd expect a significant increase in new customers or revenue to call this a success.

Alternatively, you could be testing in-app notifications to identify upsell potential. This will require little change to your existing process. You could even use a 3rd party application to start testing this. Likely a much lower increase in sales would still be a success in this scenario.

It's important to have a good understanding of your current Go-to-Market numbers. You need to know what you're comparing your results to, to make the right decisions along the journey. Make sure you know your conversion rates. Understand the different customer segments. Know how different tactics contribute to your results. This will ensure that when you start making changes, you'll view the results in the right context.

End-to-end funnel comparison

When you have a growing business, it can be hard to assess the effectiveness of PLG. In many cases, you cannot run a product-led process alongside your existing process. The mere presence of a different model will influence the effectiveness of your existing Go-to-Market, unless you are trying to address new market segments that you are not capturing today.

A good approach to get around this issue involves not announcing your product-led approach. You can only make it available to smaller segments initially. This gives you an impression of the conversion metrics in the new experience, which you can then compare to your existing approach.

To compare the output of your current growth model to any new approach, you take the number of new customers per approach and multiply this by the Lifetime Value (LTV) of customers that buy through that approach. To get the LTV, you take the Annual Contract Value (ACV) times the average contract length (in years). Then add any expansion revenue.

$$\text{New Customers (\#)} \times \left[\text{ACV (\$/yr)} \times \text{Avg Lifetime (yr)} + \text{Avg Expansion Value (\$)} \right]$$

A common challenge is that it can take one or two years to understand the full LTV in a Land and Expand approach. This is especially true when unlocking a new customer segment. You won't yet know by how much you can expand the contract and how long you will retain these customers.

A pragmatic solution for this is to look at the payback time for your Customer Acquisition Cost. In other words, to assess how long it takes to earn the marketing and sales investment back. If you can get close to or below 12 months, then you are generally looking at a good foundation. This can provide confidence to keep working on the product-led approach, even if the LTV is not clear yet.

Beyond that, you'll need to keep running experiments to validate the rest of the model, and keep updating the model as you learn more. Let's discuss how that could be done for each of the metrics in the formula.

 # New Customers

The number of new customers is typically the first metric you'll get a handle on. The impact of changes in acquisition and activation can often be measured immediately. For example, if you'd experiment with a free trial option on your website, you'll immediately see how many website visitors engage with this option. Even if they haven't signed a contract yet, this is important input to update the assumptions in your model with.

Having good analytics is key to making good decisions. Track every step of the customer journey, from page visits to button clicks and form submissions, and run experiments on each step. Try to assess the impact of intended changes before developing anything. You could for example add a button to sign up for a trial, but have sales or CS set this trial up manually on a call with the customer. This allows you to validate the interest in a free trial before developing the full self-serve experience.

This can give you a good sense of the number of new customers to expect from a product-led approach. If you apply PLG only for Retention and Expansion, then the number of new customers will of course remain unchanged.

Annual Contract Value

Once you start closing deals from your product-led approach, you'll get a sense of the ACV. Product-led approaches are typically part of a higher velocity Go-to-Market motion, so you would expect first ACV values to appear within the first 2-3 months of launching a new approach.

That doesn't mean that you have to wait for that period to pass. Keep an eye on leading indicators of contract value. These include usage within the product and the number of seats a company is using or anything else that drives your pricing. This can already provide you with early evidence to update your model with.

If you've introduced a new pricing option, you'll need to understand the new ACV. You'll want to keep an eye on the original deals your company was closing and whether those are still coming in. Is the new approach complementary, or does it cannibalize existing revenue?

When looking at this, keep an eye on the different customer segments. If lower ACV customers are from a new customer segment, this is likely a positive outcome but beware if you are seeing a lower ACV from your existing segment. That loss in revenue will have to be made up for by for example a higher number of new customers.

Average Lifetime

If you haven't made changes to your pricing model, then you could assume that retention will remain the same. That is, until you learn otherwise. A good way to assess if you should expect change in retention is to compare the product behavior. See if the new customers show different product behavior than your existing ones. If they are similar, then there's a good chance that retention behavior will be similar. If you are seeing lower activity or less users, this could be an indicator that the new segment has lower retention.

If you have introduced a new contract term then you can also expect change. A monthly self-serve plan will have a lower average lifetime than your annual deals. This would of course only be desirable if you can sell to a larger number of customers or a segment that wasn't buying before.

Expansion Revenue

Expansion revenue is the hardest metric to get a handle on, yet it's crucial to understand in a Land and Expand strategy. It's not uncommon for a larger customer to first buy a smaller contract. They might do this before deciding to onboard the entire company. Some vendors even have an intentional focus on selling \$10k to \$20k contracts at high velocity, and then upsell \$200k expansion deals to a subgroup. This happens long after they've been onboarded.

Ignoring expansion revenue could skew the value of a product-led motion but it's also not a realistic expectation to have to wait for a year or longer to understand this metric. Luckily there are some things you can do to gain more early confidence on this metric.

You could look at the contracted revenue in your existing model for a baseline value. Even when the PLG model starts at a lower ACV, you know that you can grow at least some of these customers to that value. As long as you are selling to the same segment.

You would take your current ACV after expansion and deduct the product-led new business ACV from this amount. The result is the upside you know you can capture per customer, even if the starting point is lower. Let's say you can grow your current customers to a $70k annual contract and with PLG you get customers with a $15k initial contract. Then you know that there is $55k upsell potential.

Keep in mind that these are just estimates. Customers can behave differently in a product-led approach, still these numbers will be more relevant to your business than any industry averages.

If you have a sizable customer base today, then a good approach can be to implement Product-Led Expansion first before any other product-led approaches. This allows you to get a more reliable metric of how you could upsell to customers within the product. It's often straightforward to implement and usually easy to combine with your existing approach.

This will allow you to collect real values on what product-led expansion looks like with your customers, even before applying PLG further in your Go-to-Market. After this step, you can use the above method to combine this value with any further changes you intend to make.

Follow the data

PLG is only the right choice if the results are actually better. Don't introduce a cheaper plan if it unintentionally cannibalizes your existing revenue and don't introduce a free trial if it results in fewer customers engaging with your business. Run tests and look at the data before making big decisions.

You might assume that you will close more deals of a lower value with PLG but that's not always the case. The specifics of your business and market matter. In some cases it can actually be better to sell the full contract upfront.

For example, if every buying decision has to go through a complex decision-making process, you will not want to repeat this process within months of closing the first contract. A traditional sales approach that maximizes initial contract value may be a better fit.

Therefore it's important to define your goals, run experiments and look at the numbers. Don't just assume that PLG or sales will be better.

Interview with Leah Tharin

Leah's ProducTea

The sales paradigm shift

"There's usually a heavy misalignment between sales, product, customer success and marketing because sales has probably traditionally been using the product as an acquisition machine."

- LEAH THARIN

About Leah Tharin

Leah is a leading Product-Led Growth advisor for scaling B2B companies and Interim CPGO of GotPhoto. She led products like Jua and the core product at Smallpdf with over 50 million monthly active users. She is a program creator, lecturer, executive coach and a portfolio growth advisor to VC funds like Notion Capital. She publishes guides and writes about her experiences on her blog where you can also find her podcast Leah's ProducTea.

Main takeaways

- Not all product usage indicates an intention to buy. It's important to distinguish real buying signals from mere engagement metrics. Else you risk misjudging lead quality.
- Free trials or freemiums as a model need to be considered carefully and pricing and compensation plans of the sales team need to be aligned to make this a success.

- Leverage PLG and AI to optimize sales efficiency. Avoid overloading sales teams with too many leads. Focus instead on qualifying high-potential prospects effectively.
- To enhance sales effectiveness, sales teams need enriched data about their leads before making contact. This includes product usage as well as external firmographic data.
- Product growth and sales have traditionally been seen as separate functions. Today there's a growing trend towards integrating them.

The full interview is available
as a write-up, podcast, and video.
www.PLGandSales.com/interviews

Reaching new customers in your market

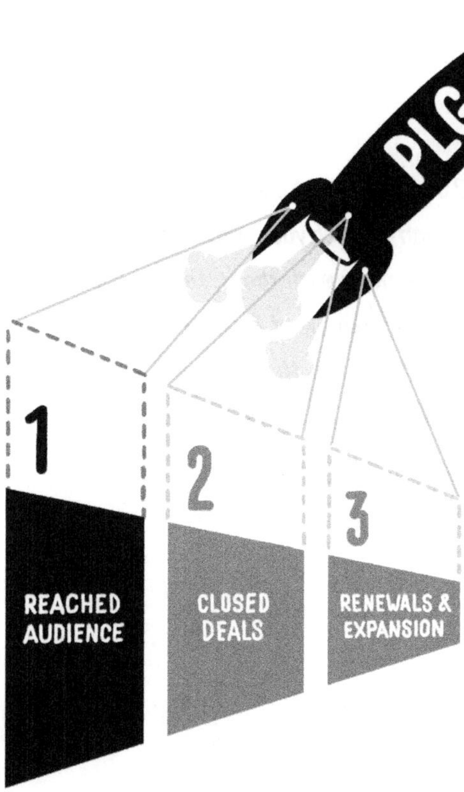

Product-Led Acquisition: Gaining new customers

When I speak with people about PLG, the first thing they typically ask is how PLG can help them reach a wider audience. It's one of the most powerful applications of PLG, as it can become the main driver of growth for a business. Companies who are successful at this also tend to reach a wide audience and through that get a lot of publicity. Stories of companies like Zoom and Slack are what comes to mind when people think of PLG. In this chapter I'll discuss the first approach to reaching new customers: Product-Led Acquisition.

PRODUCT-LED ACQUISITION (PLA)

PLA is an approach in which your product's users invite others to become users along with them, so that they can use it together. Think for example of Zoom: when you share a conference link with someone, that invites them to create their own account. Similarly, Slack encourages you to invite your colleagues, so you can communicate through Slack.

The difference between acquisition and marketing

There are two main ways to reach a wider audience through PLG. In this part I focus on the first one: Product-Led Acquisition (PLA). Before I continue, I want to clarify the difference with the second approach: Product-Led Marketing. People often mix them up in conversations and while they have similarities, they are fundamentally different.

When I talk about PLA, then the product interaction directly leads to a new user signing up for the product. This new user starts their own customer journey experience. They often experience first value in the product soon after signing up because they access the content that was being shared with them when they were invited. Growth from PLA typically comes without a time delay or human interference. The acquisition of the new user is tied to the existing user's experience and is automated. So each converted PLA interaction results in a new lead which in turn can generate revenue.

When I talk about Product-Led Marketing (PLM), then

the user of the product brings the company's brand or product in front of a new audience. The main difference is that PLM doesn't require the recipient to become a user. Think for example of filling out a form or survey someone shared or a contract that you've been asked to sign digitally. Those often include the branding of the provider but you don't need to create a user to engage. Therefore the impact is different.

Leveraging trust and relevance

PLA happens when a user of a product invites colleagues, business contacts, or friends to the application. They do this so that they can get more value out of the solution themselves. As a company grows, PLA increases in strength through network effects. Even if someone doesn't respond to the first invite, they are more likely to do so as more people invite them.

These invitations are effective because they come from someone the recipient knows, so they are not considered spam. The sender is typically trusted. That's very different from a general marketing message or an email from a sales rep, leading to higher open rates and conversion rates.

In addition, the invite comes with relevant context. It's typically an invitation to join a conversation or access content that is being shared. To be able to get access, they will have to sign up as a user. This relevant context is another driver of conversion in such a scenario. Trust and relevance are what makes a potential customer want to engage with your company and a good PLA approach includes both.

User invites

When a company uses PLA, user invites are a common tactic. Think of someone who invites you to a Zoom call or a Slack conversation. This user is asking someone who trusts them to join them and work together on the software they are using. With every new user, the value for existing users increases, creating a positive network effect.

User invites can also be implemented in the form of a referral program. The early days of Dropbox are a famous example of this. A user would receive more storage if they would invite other users, but in this promotion these accounts didn't interact with each other.

The referral approach can have many of the same growth benefits. Yet the positive impact on the existing user's experience is limited. Getting extra storage is a value that happens once, whereas being able to collaborate with people on Zoom or Slack has a recurring value.

Still, no matter if it's for collaboration or referral, user invites are a powerful way to drive growth. Either to acquire new customers or to grow the account of existing ones.

Identifying a good use-case

While PLA is a powerful approach to growth, it's not a natural fit for every company. This depends on the nature of the product your company offers. Products that are a natural fit for PLA are collaboration or communication tools. They facilitate an interaction that requires the other party to have an account. Think of the Slack and Zoom examples.

But other scenarios can also work well. The Dropbox example is often classified as a referral program, but I would say it is more than that. Dropbox intentionally designed a free experience with storage limits and they allowed users who were not ready to pay to increase this limit by inviting new people. An approach like this works best with products that have a broad audience, like cloud storage, because conversion rates are expected to be lower.

Some categories are not a natural fit for PLA. Take for example bookkeeping software. This is generally an internal tool for a few people in the company. Or CRM software, which face the challenge that sales teams don't want to make their contacts aware of any software they use. In those cases it can be harder to come up with a good approach to PLA but it's not impossible. It depends on the specifics of your company, product and customer base.

Let's take CRM software as an example. Normally there is no incentive for a CRM user to expose their relationships and deals to another company but this can be different if you look into specific verticals. In 2014 a company called Affinity launched a CRM specifically for investors. They found that investors are willing to share their networks and active deals. It helps them find opportunities to co-invest and provide introductions. So they introduced functionality for investors to connect their networks and pipeline on Affinity. Those that weren't using Affinity yet, now had an incentive to start using it. This became a driver of growth for the company within that vertical.

Whether PLA is a good fit depends on the use-case you offer, the specifics of your target audience, and your market. It's worthwhile to think creatively, but don't force it. PLA usually comes with a significant investment and if the use case is not natural, then the chances of high conversion and therewith success are lower. Think of your customer and ask yourself if there is truly added value and whether this applies for both the person who sends the invite as well as the recipient in the scenario you have in mind.

Last but not least, make sure that the person who is being invited is also a potential customer for your company. Only gaining new users who then churn immediately will not make your company successful. Some of them need to fit the customer segment you focus on. Implementing PLA is an investment. If you can find a natural use case, then this can become a strong driver for growth and will be worth considering.

Moving towards an automated journey

At the time of the Dealfront merger, many people in the software industry were talking about how Slack, Zoom, and Figma managed to grow at insane rates. They did this through viral growth loops, by encouraging users to invite people or to promote the brand to their network. It resulted in a continuous cycle (i.e. loop) of new customers finding these businesses.

At that point in time none of our products, from either Echobot or Leadfeeder, included viral growth loops. We had mechanisms to help our customers invite the rest of their team but there was no functionality that would make new customers discover our products.

We were all interested in these kinds of growth drivers for the new combined business but we concluded that this was further away from realization than other opportunities. Anyway, we first needed to do the work on onboarding and analytics. This would put us in a much better place to engage on the PLA path subsequently. So we postponed our plans for viral growth loops in favor of things that would have a more immediate business impact.

A PLA strategy can only really be successful when it's combined with further automation. For example, self-serve onboarding is a prerequisite for the acquisition to truly take off. That's because it takes the human element (or bottleneck) out of the onboarding step. People who get invited to join Slack, Zoom, or any other application, can go there and sign up immediately. They don't need to go through a sales process or a setup call first.

Without self-serve onboarding, the sales team could end up with a large volume of low intent leads. These won't convert well and the approach might therewith not be economically viable. In addition, when a user starts through self-serve, they often expect the experience to continue like that. Making the rest of the customer journey product-led can therefore amplify PLA results.

Product-Led Marketing: Having customers promote your brand

Another way to use PLG to reach a wider audience is to use it for marketing purposes. I refer to this as Product-Led Marketing (PLM). Similar to PLA, this approach leverages the product to present your brand and value proposition to new potential customers. The main difference is that with PLM, the audience is not required to become a user to engage. Instead, it makes the audience aware of your offering and how it could be of use to them, in case they have a similar need in the future.

PLM leverages the same trust dynamics as PLA. By sharing your product with their network, a user is implicitly endorsing your brand and they are showing how the product can be used. PLM can also leverage network effects. When it reaches a certain scale, people keep encountering the brand. Then even those who didn't want to try it the first time start wondering what they are missing out on.

PRODUCT-LED MARKETING

With PLM, the users of a product share the brand and product with their network. The scheduling tool Calendly is a good example. The recipient doesn't have to become a user to book the meeting, but they do see the Calendly brand throughout the scheduling experience. So, when they need a scheduling page themselves, they'll likely think of Calendly.

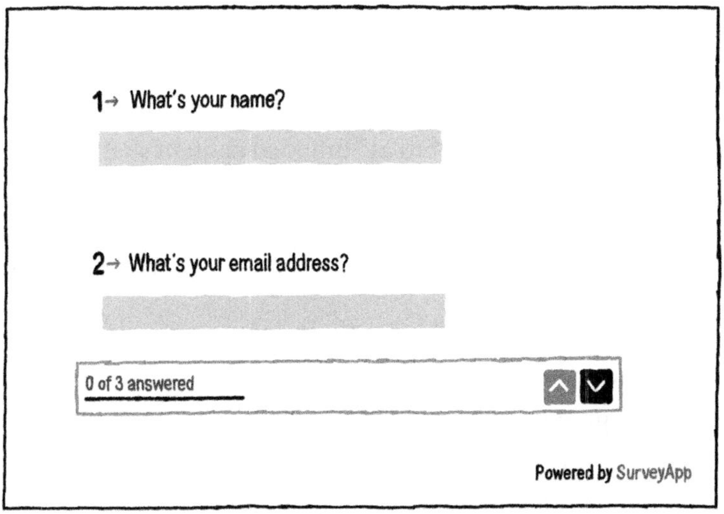

The oldest product-led trick in the book

Companies were putting their brands on products long before there was software. It's especially popular amongst sports and luxury brands. Think of any sports gear or luxury brand bags. The people who wear it are promoting this brand wherever they go. These brands then get celebrities to wear their products, which makes the people who admire them buy the products and feel more like them.

In software, this approach to growth was first adopted by consumer applications. Think of the famous Hotmail example. They offered free email accounts, but every email sent would have "Sent with Hotmail" at the bottom. In the early days of Instagram, any post shared from Instagram to Facebook would show that it was shared with Instagram.

For a while, PLM was known as "going viral". This is also where the "viral coefficient" lends its name from. Nowadays, virality is seen as a sub-component of a complete growth model like Product-Led Sales.

Branded content sharing

There is a product-led version of what the sports and luxury brands do. It's what I refer to as "branded content sharing". This is when your product enables the user to share their content with others, with your brand on it. This can be either to fulfill a transaction or to broadcast information.

A good example of this tactic is Typeform, which offers forms and surveys that are branded when on the free plan, or Docusign with its branded experience to sign documents. Often when this tactic is applied, this is done as part of a freemium model. The product can be used for free, but the "price" of this usage is that the company's brand will be included when sharing with others. There are companies that will still include their brand on some of their paid tiers as well, like is for example the case with Docusign.

Most customers don't have a problem with this branding. It allows them to access the solution at a lower price point by accepting this. For those that want to get rid of the branding, different plans are available to enable this.

Branded content sharing doesn't bring the same direct conversion as user invites but it can still have huge potential in PLG. A good application can create a growth loop where more usage of the product drives more new users into the onboarding funnel.

User-generated content

Another common tactic in PLM is to leverage the content which users create to rank better on search engines. As a company's customer base grows, its users will create more content. This will give the platform more exposure through SEO, and enable it to attract even more users.

Examples of this are user reviews on products or locations. These provide recent content and social proof, both of which help with search engine ranking. With every review, relevant content gets added to the product. The reviews might even show directly in the search results.

Zapier is a great B2B example that grew their SEO ranking through a user-generated content strategy. Zapier is an integration platform where companies add their application to connect with other software. Every time this happens, multiple pages get created.

(1) a page for the application.
(2) a page for every combination of this application with another compatible application on Zapier.
(3) a page for the available "Zaps" or triggers and actions this integration offers.

This strategy has led to tens of thousands of pages. All with relevant content for users who are looking to integrate application X with application Y. It's been an important driver of customers to the Zapier website.

Other examples of PLG that leverage user-generated content include any kind of content platform. Think of website or blog solutions that show their own logo on your pages when you are on a free plan. There are many ways to make this work. Both as a core driver of growth or as a supportive motion next to other growth tactics.

The value of prosumers

Generally, applications where the user needs to send, share, request or publish something are well suited for PLM. Some companies applying PLM also serve professionals in individual capacity ("prosumers"). This allows them to reach a much wider audience through PLM than if they only served companies with more than 50 employees. The brand value a company builds up with prosumer accounts can in turn make it easier to close deals within larger companies. More people will be familiar with the brand and software.

A good example of this is again scheduling solution Calendly. The company has a strong B2B offering, yet also prosumers who frequently need to schedule meetings often sign up for a free account. They benefit from their own free scheduling page with the Calendly brand included. While this segment costs the company money, it's getting their brand in front of potential new customers every day and some of these prosumers also have roles at the larger business Calendly wants to sell to. I have seen the effect of this first-hand at larger companies. They sometimes even refer to the scheduling use-case as "a Calendly link" regardless of if it's provided by Calendly or not.

Picking the right audience

A common pattern with PLM is that the branding and promotion gets applied to the lower or free pricing tiers. As customers pay more, they expect this advertisement to be removed. This often makes sense for two reasons. First, these tiers are a wider audience, which with PLM is what you are aiming for. Second, paying B2B customers often want their own branding on materials they send to their customers.

There are still many variations of this on the market. Website builder Webflow only brands websites on the free tier with a "Made with Webflow" badge. Yet DocuSign's brand remains visible on their lowest priced plan. My theory is that it's just more common and accepted for e-signing solutions to come with branding, since other providers in the space are doing the same.

When to remove the advertisement is as much art as it is science. It depends what your customers are used to and what alternatives there are on the market. Other important factors are your pricing model and related to that, how much value the customer is getting by accepting to promote your brand.

There is no silver bullet for this but keep in mind that this is a marketing approach. Success is therefore measured through marketing metrics. Assess if you are reaching the right audience, how much of that audience you are reaching and measure conversion of your efforts, even if it's indirect. PLM is often a larger investment that can take time to pay off. So metrics like this will make sure you stay focused on the desired outcome.

Interview with Japna Sethi

Calendly

Finding your place on the PLG and Sales spectrum

"Sometimes you need those human calories to land a deal because it's a larger customer, or maybe it's a very complex product, or there's multiple decision makers in the process."

- JAPNA SETHI

About Japna Sethi

Japna is currently a Product and Growth leader at Calendly. Before this she has led Product Growth in a number of well-known companies. For example, she was a lead for Product and Growth at Dropbox and she built and led the Growth team at Productboard from the ground up. She is based out of San Francisco and also advises and invests in companies that need help with their growth.

Main takeaways

- Testing should involve a portfolio approach with various hypotheses and strategies. It should balance short-term experiments with long-term bets.
- Support teams can evolve into profit centers by assisting users and guiding them through conversion processes. This drives conversion and revenue generation.
- It's crucial to give strategies sufficient time to succeed or

fail before moving on to the next approach. Else teams end up circling back to the same ideas over and over.

- It's essential to ensure that you have product-market fit before focusing on scaling growth strategies like PLG. Jumping into growth initiatives too early can be counterproductive.
- PLG and traditional sales are not binary options; rather, they exist on a spectrum. Companies should assess where they lie on this spectrum and adapt their strategies accordingly.

The full interview is available
as a write-up, podcast, and video.
www.PLGandSales.com/interviews

Engaging and converting your audience

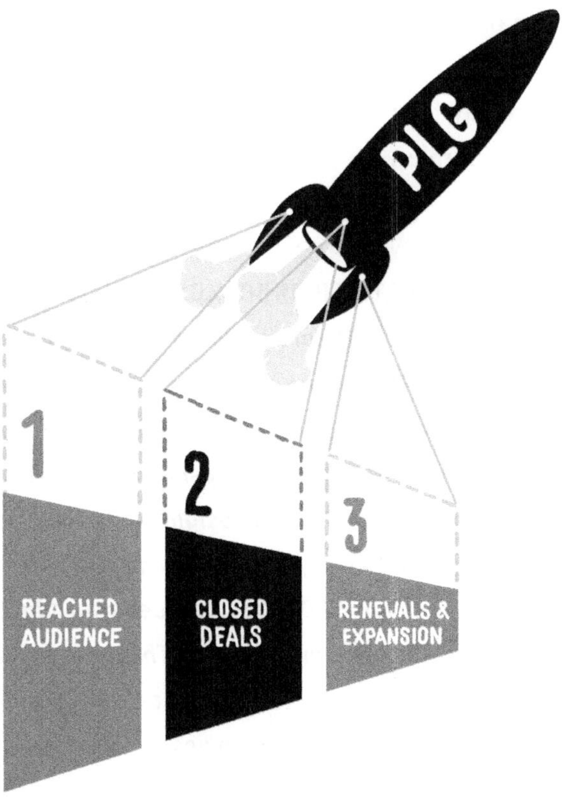

Product-Led Onboarding: Enabling customers to get started

In a product-led approach, a customer can often start using a software product without speaking with anybody at the company that sells it. This Product-Led Onboarding (PLO) is one of the most characterizing traits of PLG.

The steps to convert a customer from initial interest to active user of the product are fundamentally different. Companies using traditional sales often require a customer to sign a contract in order to get access. A product-led experience, on the other hand, delivers value first, and only then asks the customer to pay. The good thing is, this approach can also be combined with sales.

PRODUCT-LED ONBOARDING (PLO)

PLO is an intuitive self-service approach for a new user to get started with your product. A well-known application of this approach is to offer a self-serve freemium or free trial of your product. Companies applying PLA or PLM, like Slack, Zoom, and Docusign, all do this, but it can also be applied when you are reaching your audience through paid ads or SEO. The Leadfeeder product at Dealfront is a good example of this. The product itself doesn't bring in new customers, but the trial allows people to get started by themselves.

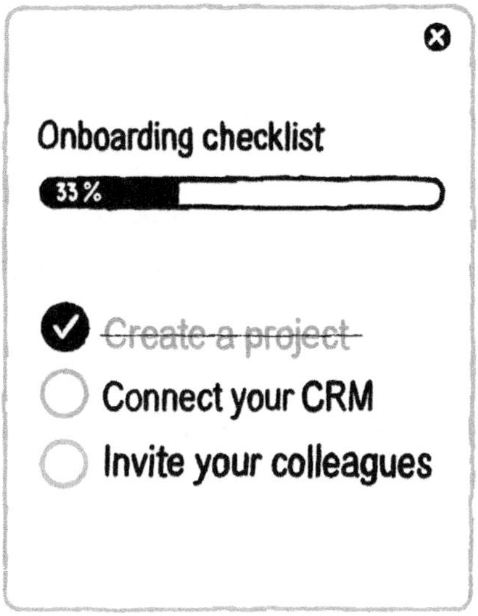

Customers don't want to wait

Let's say a potential customer has done their research. They have identified your product as a possible solution to their problem. At this point, they don't want to be slowed down by your organizational process. Let's discuss three common scenarios and analyze how they affect the customer experience.

Imagine a customer is on your website and ready to take the next step and engage with your business. Here's what could happen next:

1. Traditional sales - How it used to be

In a traditional sales approach there would usually be a "Contact Sales" or "Book a demo" button on the website. This would bring the user to a form to collect their details for a call. After submitting the form, the customer gets a "We'll be in touch shortly" type of message. The lead then gets routed and assigned to a sales rep, who gets in touch as soon as possible by email to find a time. This can take five minutes or five days and the customer doesn't know what's happening in the background. So they often continue to look for a solution elsewhere.

2. Traditional sales - The modern approach

Luckily sales automation has come a long way in the past 10 years. Many companies now automatically route the lead to the right sales rep upon form submission. They can then immediately show the calendar with the sales rep's availability and the customer can schedule an appointment for their call. This takes away the customer's uncertainty about when the meeting will take place, but they will still need to wait for the call to happen.

3. Product-Led Onboarding

In this scenario, access to the product is fully automated. The website will have a "Start a Free Trial" or "Get Started for Free" button. A few details need to be filled out to create an account and then the user is in the product without delays. An onboarding tour or other intuitive pointers within the product help the customer to use the product in the right way. There could still be an option to speak with the sales team but at this point the customer has already seen first value. So they enter that conversation with a completely different mindset.

As you can see, the waiting time experienced by the customer is quite different per scenario. In the first scenario, the customer doesn't know when they will hear back. In the second scenario, they might have a date and time, but it's unlikely to be within the next five minutes.

There is a continuous flow of research emphasizing the importance of the response time to customers. An online search for "speed to lead statistics" will guide you to the latest articles. Clearly the 'time to contact a lead' is a key driver for success. So the last thing you to do when a customer has shown interest to engage, is to make them wait. This is leaving the door wide open for more agile competitors to take your spot.

Product-Led Onboarding can help with this. By enabling the customer to explore the product, they get more engaged with your company. This will also buy you some time to allow the right person to get in touch with them. While the customer is setting up the product, an onboarding specialist could be assigned. They could reach out by phone, email or through in-app chat to start a conversation. In the other two scenarios, the customer will have left your website having submitted the demo request. They could either be exploring alternatives or doing something else entirely.

Offering a free version: the Freemium model

One of the most well-known PLG models is the freemium. The freemium model involves a free plan in your pricing model. This plan is available for any customer to use, typically for an unlimited period of time. This free plan has limited feature capabilities. It gives the company market exposure or keeps potential customers engaged with the product when they are not ready to buy yet.

Companies that apply viral growth loops typically offer some kind of freemium model. This is because even a free user helps to get their brand and product in front of further potential customers. It basically becomes a marketing expense. In usage-based pricing models it is also a common approach as it removes friction from getting people to use it in the first place. It allows the user to get to value without friction and ideally they develop a first habit.

Try before you buy: Trials

Another well-known model for onboarding is the free trial. In a free trial, a company offers full access to their product for a limited period of time. This approach is today used by companies like Shopify, Zendesk, and Intercom. In a true product-led motion these free trials are initiated through self-serve onboarding but a free trial can also be offered by a sales rep following a product demo.

The goal of a trial is to make the customer more confident that your solution solves their problem. That means that the length of your trial needs to be long enough for them to experience this value. Most trials are between 1 week and 1 month of length, with 2 weeks being the most common.

If it takes longer for your customers to see the value, considering a paid pilot might be worth it. Alternatively, if these customers provide brand exposure or access to data, then a freemium would be a better fit.

In case you are wondering whether to start with a freemium or a free trial, there's a third option: the reverse trial. In a reverse trial, a company offers a free trial with full functionality. If the user doesn't convert by the end of the trial, they fall back to a free version of the product.

This combines the best of both worlds. Users enjoy the full experience for a limited time. If your product has delivered value, then you'll have a good chance to convert them to a paying customer. For customers who are not ready to buy, the fallback to freemium allows you to keep them engaged. They can use the free version until they might be ready to buy.

This model is used by companies like Calendly and Amplitude. We also use it for our Leadfeeder product at Dealfront. During the trial a user has all features enabled and can identify an unlimited number of companies on their website. On the free plan functionality is limited and we only show a subset of the identified companies. Some companies stay on the free plan for months or even years before they become a paying customer.

Focus on delivering value

When a new customer signs up for your product, those first moments are all about showing value. You want to get the customer to their "aha moment". This is the first moment the user sees that your product can actually solve their problem. So if you include an onboarding tour or checklist, you want to focus this on driving value for the customer. Your aim is not to show them the entire product you've built. You want them to see how this will make their life better. If you can do that by showing them only 10% of the product, then focus only on that 10%. Any distractions from the main goal will result in users dropping off because they will think that this is not solving their problem.

A great example of this is how Canva offers specific journeys for different use-cases. For example, one of the use-cases they offer is design for social media content. If I'm looking for this use-case, then I will likely land on use-case specific pages on their website. These pages will have targeted content and a more specific button that says "Design for Social Media", instead of something more general like "Get Started for Free". Once I sign up for the product, I'm taken to the social media templates and can start creating my first visual right away. It's that simple. Canva serves so much more than just that social media use-case but they keep the experience laser-focused. This prevents confusion and gives the customer what they are looking for.

Interactive demos

If your product is not ready for self-serve, you could consider an Interactive Demo. This option has become more popular in recent years. Instead of full access to your product, an Interactive Demo provides a guided introduction. The user follows a preconfigured product experience. It gives them a feeling for what the product looks like and what capabilities it might offer. The demo is typically created using a 3rd party platform such as Reprise or Demoboost.

We implemented this approach for our Sales Intelligence products at Dealfront. Historically, new customers for these products were onboarded by our implementation team, so it was unlikely that letting users in to explore by themselves would bring us the best results. Customers would struggle to figure out our most competitive features.

We were working on making this experience more intuitive. In the meantime, the Interactive Demo allowed us to take an immediate step into the direction of PLG. We provided the demo on our website for new customers and showed it within the platform for existing customers of other products. It's a product-led way to introduce them to the other solutions we offer.

Changing the sales mindset

Some people think that applying PLO means you won't need a sales team anymore, but that's not true. A sales team that reaches out to qualified customers during onboarding can have a lot of value. As we discussed in the section on Sales Assist, the best way to engage a customer in this scenario is different from traditional sales. You'll want to guide the user through the product experience and help them get to value.

If your company is used to traditional sales, then introducing PLO requires a change in mindset. You won't want to contact every lead by phone as soon as possible anymore. You'll want to let new customers onboard themselves and qualify their product usage. This means the company starts using customer behavior as a segmentation metric. The Sales Assist team will reach out to customers who are getting enough value. Only these customers are qualified as leads for sales.

Product-Led Qualification: Identifying good-fit customers

One of the key applications of PLG for Go-to-Market efficiency is customer qualification. This approach enables you to identify companies with a much higher likelihood to buy, so you can focus your sales resources there and increase your conversion rates.

Traditionally, lead qualification has been driven by customer characteristics. Think of company firmographics, such as industry, employee size, and revenue, as well as the demographics of the contact person, such as location, job title, and tenure. These days, B2B companies often include further layers, such as recent events that might signal that this customer is in the market for a solution. Examples are new hires, recent funding or geographic expansion. The goal is to assign resources towards the leads that are most likely to convert.

A product-led way of qualifying customers is by looking at their product data. This is called Product-Led Qualification (PLQ). You assign leads who have taken qualifying actions within the product. Those we call Product Qualified Leads (PQLs). Beyond user behavior, PLQ can include information entered by the customer, such as the details of a job post or a project. It can also be data that's being processed from a connected calendar, CRM, or an imported file. What data you'll have available is specific to your product and company.

PRODUCT-LED QUALIFICATION (PLQ)

PLQ involves measuring the product usage of users and teams and using that data for qualification. Based on this segmentation, the company might decide to deploy the sales team, or to provide the user with specific offers within the application or by email. At Leadfeeder, a Product-Qualified Lead is someone who has installed the tracking script on their website. At this point the product can identify the companies that visit their website. This makes it much more likely that we can provide value to the customer.

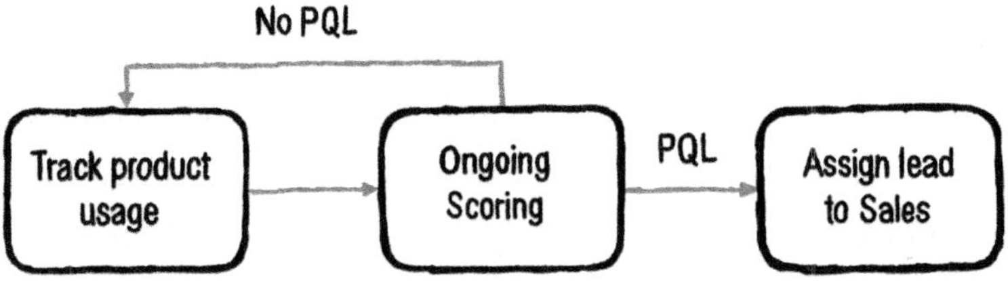

Letting the product qualify your leads

PLQ differs in two ways from how leads are qualified in traditional sales. In PLQ, unqualified leads can continue to use the product. They won't know that they were not qualified as a customer. They might even purchase the product through self-service or they might request a quote from sales if they are ready to buy (so-called "hand raisers"). In traditional sales an unqualified lead rarely has any other way to engage with the company.

Secondly, in traditional sales the qualification usually happens once. PLQ tends to happen more than once. If a company has a freemium model, they might re-qualify all accounts on a daily or weekly basis. In a free trial, there may be multiple moments that trigger re-qualification. Let's say a user invites five team members to join them. This might immediately move them to the PQL segment if this is a key behavior for your company.

Which brings us to another important characteristic of qualification in B2B. It's important to assess the qualification based on the behavior of a team. Don't only look at a single user. Often a business user will need to onboard their colleagues to get real value from a product, for example to drive collaboration or communication. Qualification criteria should therefore be measured and assessed at team or company level.

But what exact behavior are we looking for when defining a PQL? This depends on the specifics of a company's onboarding and Go-to-Market approach. It should help you decide when to either push a promotion to get a customer to buy or when to engage a sales rep to drive further conversion. It's something to experiment with on a regular basis. The only rule to remember is that a PQL is more than just a signup. The user should have completed certain key onboarding steps. Often they'll have experienced a first moment of value from your product.

What to do when a lead becomes a PQL

In the same way that definitions of PQLs can differ, there is also no set rule defining how they should be handled. A company could have different PQL definitions for different scenarios. Such as winning a new customer, expanding within a use-case, or selling another product. For each of these scenarios the handling of a PQL could be different. For new customers, it might be that sales reaches out once a new user becomes a PQL. While for the expansion within a use-case you might show an in-app message. You could allow customers to do this through self-service.

The decision of what tactic to apply to a PQL comes down to the Return On Investment. For a new customer, the impact on revenue could be sufficient to engage a sales team. But when an existing customer wants to add a few users, that may not be profitable. The value increase may not make the investment of a sales rep's time worthwhile, so an automated approach could fit better here.

The goal is to reach out at the right time and to let the product do the initial heavy lifting. To move to PLQ you will need to build confidence in two directions:

1. **The onboarding process.** This process needs to be able to get new users through the right steps when starting to use the product.
2. **The qualification process.** The qualification based on behavior needs to result in higher closing rates or higher contract values.

When you introduce PLQ, you are telling the sales team to not reach out to new leads who are signing up for the product. You are going to wait and monitor the product usage and only a subset of those signups who took qualifying actions will be provided to the sales team. These should be much better leads, but that will need to be proven first. It will feel unnatural to the sales team to let leads sit there and if the process doesn't work well, the company risks losing good leads and revenue. This might be the case if the product is too hard to use, if the required learning curve takes too long or if the onboarding process is not mature enough.

Also beware that an automated qualification process may not always behave as intended. Especially in the beginning, you need to regularly assess the success of each part of the process. Certain assumptions may not hold over time. I've also seen cases where the enrichment of an important field of customer data didn't always succeed. This resulted in large sets of good customers not getting qualified as a result. So always keep your eye on the unqualified leads. Validate regularly that this is indeed a group of customers your company does not want to spend more resources on.

When implementing this, I recommend an open dialogue with the sales team. Give them the opportunity to point out parts of the process that seem suboptimal. Your sales team knows best how to sell to your customers and they know which narratives drive success in the sales process. In my view, PLQ cannot be implemented in isolation without the involvement of the sales team.

Combining the best of both worlds

If you do traditional sales today, then you should have a good sense of which leads are a good fit, independent of their product usage. To de-risk your PLG efforts, you won't want to go all-in on PLQ right away. Luckily, there are good ways to combine the two.

For example, you can use PLQ as a primary qualifier. In this case you would still reach out to high value customer segments proactively, regardless of their product usage. For example, any company with more than 200 employees or in a certain industry could be assigned a sales rep. This way you won't risk losing these important accounts and it gives time to prove the value of this process on the other customer segments.

Still, it's important to give the product-led process a chance to deliver in the majority of the cases. This way ensures you are learning the right things to improve. In the above scenario, this could mean that the sales team reaches out a little later than usual. Having the original process as a fallback can be a good safety net until you are more confident about the qualification process.

Getting qualification right requires a leap of faith from the old ways to the new product-led way. It's important therefore to make decisions based on data and real-life examples and to keep an open dialogue with the sales team as you develop this approach.

Product-Led Conversion: Allowing customers to buy

In a product-led buying process the customer receives value before deciding to buy. The emphasis is on closing the initial deal as fast as possible, focused on the use-case in which the customer has shown interest. As part of this experience, it's often possible to pay for the product through self-service. We refer to this as Product-Led Conversion (PLC) and it provides another way for customers to buy your product next to speaking with the sales team.

PRODUCT-LED CONVERSION (PLC)

PLC happens when a new customer can buy your product without needing to speak with someone in your company. Most companies that identify themselves as product-led have PLC in place, even if they also have a Sales Assist team for certain customer segments. PLC can help acquire new customers and/or expand contracts.

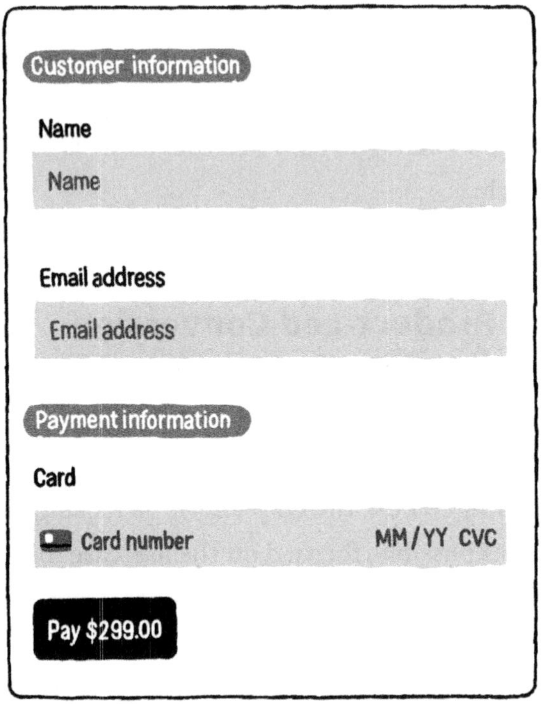

Choosing speed over initial contract value

It can be challenging to compare the return of traditional sales with that of a Land and Expand approach. The sales team may raise concerns that moving to a PLC model could have significant opportunity cost because they were able to close larger deals with the same customers. These concerns can be valid, so you'll need to run experiments to figure out the best model.

As we've seen, this is not an easy analysis to make. You can't just compare the initial deal sizes. At the same time you won't yet know the conversion values of the different product-led steps of the process. Though, there are some easy indicators to show that you've uncovered business value:

- If you see more deals getting closed than before. Even if they are of lower value, it means you've found a way to access a larger audience.
- If you are selling the same volume to the same customers, but the sales team doesn't need to be involved in all of them. Then you have found a more efficient way to go to market.

There are more ways that PLC can add value to a business and this is heavily influenced by the pricing model that you are working with.

Differentiating by customer behavior

When implementing PLC it's important to consider different customer segments. Again, a good way to do that is on the basis of their behavior. You can for example segment by the channel through which a customer came in, the keywords or use-case in which they are interested or which button they clicked on the website.

A simple example of this is to offer a "Request a Demo" and "Start a Free Trial" button next to each other. This allows customers to self-qualify based on which option they prefer. I've tested this in multiple companies and often the combination results in higher total conversion rates. At the same time it directs your website visitors to their preferred experience where they can either buy from the sales team, or through self-service.

A common misconception is that demos are only for traditional or conservative buyers and that innovative buyers will want to start a trial immediately. This can be true, but there could be many other reasons why a customer may prefer a demo. For example, someone from a large organization may not be authorized to sign up before your software has been approved or an executive who is not going to use the product themselves wants to understand the value for their team. Let's say your website audience includes a meaningful executive segment. Then having an alternative path next to self-service will likely drive better results.

In most markets, both types of buyers exist. Those who prefer to speak with sales, and those who don't want to try and buy by themselves. Offering both options therefore maximizes the number of customers who can buy your product in whichever way they prefer.

Deploying a hybrid model

If you do traditional sales today, I recommend starting by adding a light product-led experience, such as an interactive demo or a trial that gets set up by your team. Don't get rid of the working sales process but start learning which approach your customers actually prefer and whether it might make sense to serve both models or if there is a clear preference for one.

This also makes the conversation with the sales team easier because you won't take away their pipeline overnight. If the data shows that more people click the trial option, then you've identified a customer preference. With this data you can further optimize your model. It will give the organization time to get used to a new way of working, build confidence, and adapt team resourcing where required.

Interview with Ben Williams

The Product-Led Geek

Navigating the intersection of sales and PLG

"Boiling the ocean is a recipe for disaster with PLG. So pick a playbook to focus on first and ignore the others for now. You'll get to them."

- BEN WILLIAMS

About Ben Williams

Ben is a Product and Growth executive and strategic advisor to startups with 20+ years of experience. In his career, he has held roles like VP of Product-Led Growth at Snyk and VP of Products at Cloudbees. Nowadays he is an advisor to founders and product/growth leaders of growth stage B2B startups. He loves all things PLG, building and scaling product and growth teams, and loop-based growth strategy. You can also follow his thoughts in his newsletter The Product-Led Geek.

Main takeaways

- Ben explains how they used the user base and product analytics to fuel the growth of the enterprise pipeline.
- He explains how the focus on bottom-up adoption was pivotal for the success of Snyk. This was driven by addressing developers' needs for security tools.
- Metrics like Product Influenced Revenue and Net Revenue Retention are crucial for assessing PLG

effectiveness. They highlight the impact of product interactions on sales outcomes.

- Ben recommends aligning PLG initiatives with business goals. He explains how to build confidence with a methodical approach, such as starting with smaller, pilot-style projects.
- Benchmarking against PLG implementations in comparable companies can provide good insights. These don't have to be competitors, but have similar operating models.

The full interview is available as a write-up, podcast, and video.
www.PLGandSales.com/interviews

Retaining and growing existing contracts

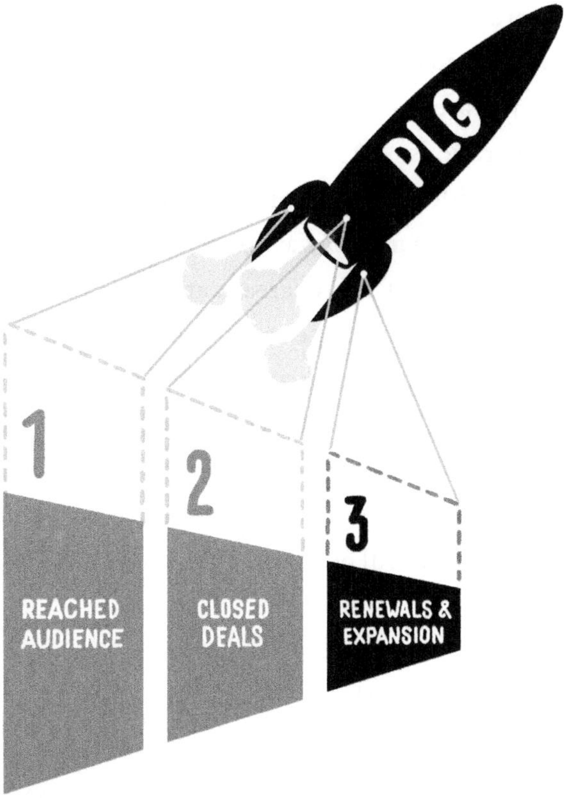

Product-Led Retention: Keeping your customers engaged

Perhaps the most established product-led approach is how Customer Success (CS) uses product data. It's not always classified as a PLG approach but in any scenario where product data becomes a core part of how a team operates, we are talking about a product-led approach.

Retention is a metric that is usually owned by CS. This focuses on the company's ability to retain customers through one or more contract renewals. CS tends to follow the same interaction-based model as in sales. Personal touchpoints with the customer are the main means to understand their needs and considerations.

The downside of this approach is that customers don't suddenly decide to move away from your product. First their usage of the product will decrease and may stop altogether, often as a result of a change in circumstances. An employee may have left or a process may have changed. It's only a few months later that a company will realize they are paying for something that is no longer delivering value. If the change in circumstance and usage could be identified earlier, then the contract may often still be saved. This is where PLG comes in.

PRODUCT-LED RETENTION (PLR)

PLR involves tracking a customer's product usage and using this data to predict contract renewal. This can be done by measuring activity levels on key actions in the product, or by keeping track of events that might signal churn, such as the main user leaving the company. You can also track key events or a customer health score and trigger automations based on those. The goal is to identify changes in usage or value at an early stage, before the customer stops using your solution.

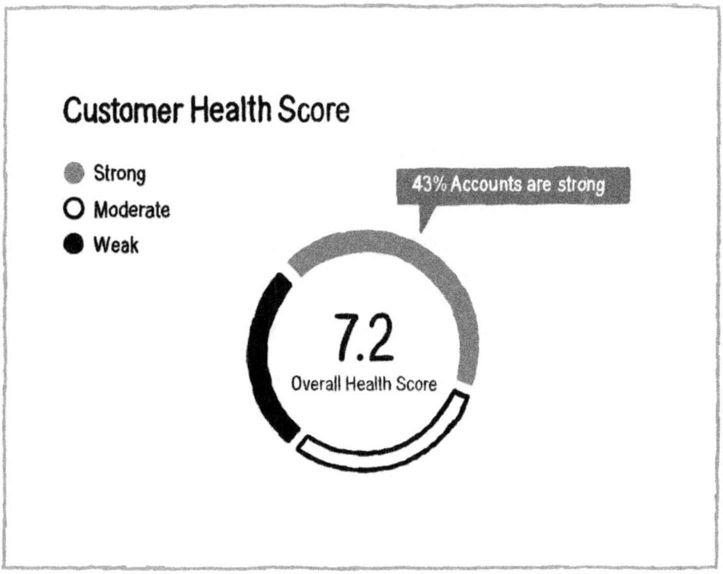

Moving from recovery to prevention

Changes in product usage can be triggered for many different reasons. For example a change in personnel or management; a change in working methods; or new tooling being adopted. To leverage the product for retention, CS needs access to usage analytics. Ideally they will want to be notified when the usage changes, if your champion stops logging in or the number of active team members is going down. These are all things your CS team should know about, so they can reach out to their point of contact and get ahead of the situation.

A change in usage doesn't have to mean that the customer can't use your product anymore but it might require you to reposition the value of your product to match the new situation. You might even have to re-sell the value altogether if your buyer has changed. By catching these events early, you reach the customer while they are still looking into the situation, so you can provide input and reengage them before any decisions are made.

Defining a health score

The good news is that it is already quite common for CS teams to work with product data. For CS software like Totango this is actually one of their core propositions. They capture these product signals and notify the CS team with the right context to engage. A common way of managing this is with a so-called 'health score'. A health score doesn't necessarily consist of product signals alone but they are usually the main component of such a score. So let's explore this concept a little more in the context of PLR.

In a typical health score, a company will try to combine a number of different signals into a single number (the score). It uses traffic light coloring to signal if a customer's account is either healthy (green light) or at risk (red light). The effectiveness of all this comes down to how the company has defined the score itself, particularly the underlying metrics around user engagement.

For example, a user could be classified as "active" on the basis of whether they have logged in to the product or by measuring if the customer is actually getting value out of the product. The latter is of course a much more reliable indicator for a health score. Yet even when assessing value, it matters how this is defined. Different customers may use your product in very different ways.

Let's say your product provides analytics or insights. Some of your users may log in every day and engage with the reports. Others may log in once a month and download all the results for analysis offline. Both sets of individuals may be very happy customers and your health score needs to be able to reflect these different usage patterns. This makes it hard to look at a single number in isolation but a health score can be a good early indicator that the customer requires investigation.

Keeping it updated

There is an art to finding the right definition of "healthy usage" for any product. To add complexity, this definition can change over time. Sometime changes are not necessarily negative but still drive a change in how customers use your product. Think for example of changes you make to your product offering or changes in the software stack that your customer uses.

It's also important to align on any definitions of customer health between Product, CS, and other key stakeholders in the business. You want to make sure all departments are using the same measurement of success. I find it useful to discuss the reports of these metrics regularly with all stakeholders at least on a monthly basis. This assures all teams have the same understanding of what's happening in the business and that they agree on what needs to be done to improve things.

It's hard for a SaaS business to be successful if you are not able to retain your customers. So use product data to identify customers who are at risk of jumping ship early on and reach out in a timely way to prevent any churn from happening.

Product-Led Expansion: Introducing new products

Once you have paying customers, there is another opportunity for PLG: Product-Led Expansion (PLE). The possibilities for this depend on your pricing and packaging. A customer may be able to buy further seats or complementary modules or you may have other products to meet further use-cases. Traditionally CS would bring this up in a quarterly review or Account Management may have identified this company as a good fit. The problem is that in neither of these scenarios the customer has actually signaled a need. PLE allows you to identify the right customer at the right time and focus your expansion efforts there.

PRODUCT-LED EXPANSION (PLE)

With PLE, you showcase expansion options within the product while customers are using it. For example, the product might suggest inviting more users to collaborate on content, display some metrics as a teaser of an analytics add-on, or point out options that can only be used on higher-value plans. The goal is to get the user interested and encourage them to explore this additional functionality. Then, they might buy it directly in the application, or request a call to discuss.

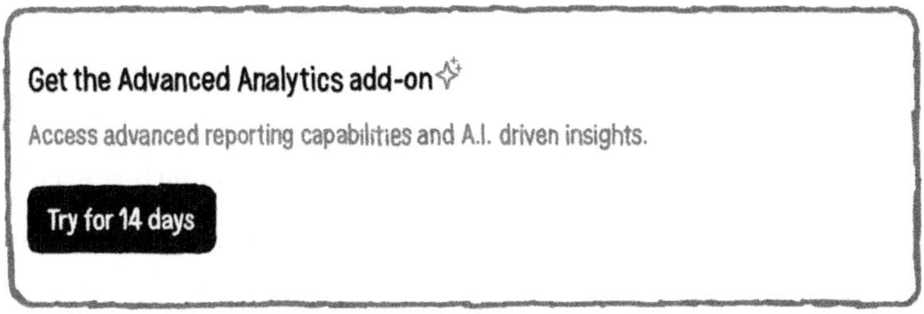

Upsell through product usage

PLE is an approach that is perfectly suited for step-by-step implementation as it doesn't require a complete change of strategy. This makes it especially interesting for companies using traditional sales. Firstly, identify the right moment at which a customer might need an additional product. Then you can start with a simple in-app notification to introduce the product and offer a call for them to learn more. Ideally, include the option for the customer to book this call, in-app, right away.

This follows the same principles as Product-Led Qualification. Once again we look at the product usage to decide on the right moment to reach out to a customer. The only difference here is that this customer already has a contract with you. If you are seeing good results, you can consider building these further into the product. For example you might introduce product previews or allow the customer to try the additional product for a limited period of time.

With your existing customers, there is a higher level of trust and you have more user context. This puts you in a favorable position to sell. You just need to identify what the customer needs. It's a great way to increase the contract value per customer.

In-app messaging

One of the more powerful instruments for expansion is in-app messaging. Once a user has signed up for your product, in-app messaging and guidance can drive many key growth metrics.

In-app messaging can actually support every step of the customer journey, from onboarding, to engagement and expansion. This kind of functionality is often provided by a third-party provider such as Pendo or Userpilot but some companies also choose to build this capability in-house.

It's all about showing contextually relevant information at the right time. Think, for example, of a product-tour once a customer has signed up for a new solution or hints provided throughout the product to explain the functionality. In the context of expansion, it can also be used to highlight new functionality or to show promotions to certain customer segments.

In-app messaging can also be the bridge between the application and a human touch. You can use it to offer a call with support or an account manager at any time this makes sense during the experience.

To do this effectively, it's important to tie the message to what the user is currently doing. Look at where the user is, in the application. What they are trying to do? You can even include specifics you already know about the user, for example, their use case preferences. The more personalized, the higher the chance of a successful outcome.

You can only use in-app messaging from the moment a user has signed up and it can be a key driver of activation, conversion to paid, and expansion. It's a powerful tool in your PLG tool chest.

Trials for paying customers

You might wonder how far you should allow a customer to go before requiring further payment. Many product-led companies offer the option of starting a free trial of an add-on module. This is similar to the onboarding and qualification of new customers. The idea is to have the product do the heavy lifting; to identify qualified customers for upselling and focus your resources on those most likely to convert.

In a fully product-led experience the customer will also be able to pay for this new add-on or product through self-service but this doesn't always make sense. In some cases, the upsell can cost more than the original contract or it can be too complex to be configured through self-service. In those cases, offering a scheduling page to book a call can be a good alternative.

What I love about PLE is that you don't need to have these in-app trials or payments in place to enjoy the benefits. The real value in PLE comes from identifying the right moment when a customer has a need and then presenting your solution for this need at that moment. Customer are often willing to join a call to get more information so even without a trial, you can still reap much of the reward of the approach, just by using in-app messages in a smart way. This is something any company could start experimenting with today and it's a great way to become more product-led.

Interview with Todd Olson

Pendo

Using in-app messaging for tailored user experiences

"If you think about it, a decent part of the humans in our Go-to-Market are teaching people how to use the product. Because people do want to try things before they buy."

- TODD OLSON

About Todd Olson

Todd Olson is the co-founder and CEO of Pendo. In 1997 he founded a data integration company called Cerebellum. Later, in 2004, he founded 6th Sense Analytics, which he sold to Rally Software and then served as their VP of Product. These experiences led him to create Pendo in 2013. Pendo has since become one of the leading providers of in-app messaging software and further products to drive business results in software products.

Main takeaways

- Todd discusses advanced implementations that personalize customer interactions by using signals from Pendo and bringing them into your CRM.
- He discusses various methods for product expansion, including natural expansion levers like seat usage thresholds and promoting new functionality through in-app marketing.

- Todd stresses the importance of adopting product-led techniques as well as leveraging AI to meet evolving user needs and remain competitive.
- The interview includes examples of how automating tasks like onboarding frees up customer-facing resources for more value-added activities.
- Companies are increasingly focused on automating customer interactions. Particularly for smaller accounts, to streamline processes and improve efficiency.

The full interview is available as a write-up, podcast, and video.
www.PLGandSales.com/interviews

Three steps to get started

1. Defining your goals

In this chapter we'll get more hands on and start defining your next steps to introduce PLG in your Go-To-Market. As is hopefully clear by now, the question isn't IF but WHERE in your existing model to start experimenting with PLG. To figure that out, we'll start by defining the goal. PLG can impact quite a few different business outcomes so we need to create clarity on what a good result looks like.

For example, the general intent of Dealfront is to become more product-led but this is not a business goal by itself. That would be like saying our goal is "to do sales". PLG is an approach that we leverage to achieve a goal, like growing new business revenue or reducing churn.

The most common business outcomes PLG can drive are:

Increase new business revenue

There are several ways PLG can help a company to generate new business revenue. The best approach depends on what your company needs. You may, for example, need more people to come to your website. This would mean we would look towards Product-Led Acquisition or Marketing. Alternatively you could need more of your existing website visitors to engage with the business. This would mean that you'd focus on Product-Led Onboarding. If you'd want new business revenue from an entirely new segment in the market, we might want to introduce an offering for small-business customers and leverage PLG for that.

Improve Go-to-Market efficiency

To improve the efficiency of your current model, you might look at Product-Led Qualification. This will lead to higher quality leads for your sales team and thus higher closing rates. Alternatively, we can also improve efficiency in other parts of the customer journey. Let's say you already have a high volume of visitors coming to your website, but you want to capture the details of more of your visitors. Offering a trial might appeal to your visitors. It could allow you to get more leads out of the same audience.

Improve retention

No matter which other goal you might pursue with PLG, it will in most cases drive user engagement. User engagement is often one of the strongest predictors for retention but there are more things to consider. You can improve activation rates by getting more new users to take key steps in the product or reactivate the users that have lost the habit of using your product. By using targeted messaging you can bring them back into the product before they decide they might not need your solution anymore.

Drive expansion revenue

You can also grow revenue by selling more to existing customers. You might want to increase the number of users per customer, increase the use of credits, or sell add-ons and other products. As with most of PLG, adoption ideally comes first and payment later. So you might realize that payment is standing in the way of usage and early value. For example if you sell more seats, you might consider to onboard the users before you ask for payment.

Before moving on to the next step, try to identify which of these 4 goals is currently the highest priority in your company. Try to go a level deeper, for example by identifying what type of new business or expansion revenue your company is trying to generate more of. Or what part of the customer journey requires attention to improve retention metrics. This can give you a good indication of where to focus your PLG efforts. We'll figure out which PLG approaches are most suitable for your business in the next step.

2. Deciding where to start

Next we want to get an idea of how well you're positioned to apply the different product-led approaches. At the end of this chapter you will find a link to a free online assessment where you can answer a few questions to figure out the best place to start introducing PLG.

Top of the funnel

Many companies looking into PLG are seeking the potential to promote their business. Either through Product-Led Acquisition or Marketing. They want to increase visibility in the market to bring in new customers.

As we know, for PLA to work well, the product needs to facilitate a certain level of collaboration. This can be when the product enables users to communicate with each or other collaborative experiences like task/project management or design reviews. It's what's making one user invite another.

For PLM to work well, the product needs to facilitate a

transaction of information or value. This can be when a user wants to share a survey with respondents, or collect payments from a customer. It can even be a message that they send to their network. Any mechanism that shares your brand to a wider audience.

If your product enables the above experiences, then you might be able to use PLG to reach a broader audience. This can be a powerful driver of new customers and revenue for the business.

Even if your product doesn't have any of this, there are still ways to drive top of the funnel impact with PLG. For example if the total addressable market in terms of users is meaningful, which for me means above 10 Million people. In that case there can still be an angle for customer acquisition or marketing through the product experience, even if there is no natural way to get users to invite others.

You could consider other tactics like releasing a new free product specifically aimed at driving brand awareness. An example would be the free Logo API that Clearbit released. Many companies included Clearbit in their applications because of this but it's not one of their core revenue drivers.

If you have a secondary audience of above 10 Million people, then that could also be an opportunity for PLG. A secondary audience for a software for doctors would be their patients. They are not the buyer but they can still help drive awareness amongst your primary audience (the doctors).

With a secondary audience the angle is slightly different though. You'll want to create an experience that attracts more people from that audience, such as patients leaving reviews for doctors. By increasing the number of patients, your relevance for the doctors will grow. You can then introduce features to connect patients with doctors. This connects the growth loop with your buyer.

It's possible that there is no form of collaboration or sharing in your product and that there is no large audience to target in any way. In that case it might be hard to drive top of the funnel growth with PLG. You can either change those conditions, which would imply a change of strategy or instead, start looking at the potential of Product-Led Onboarding and Expansion.

Go-to-Market efficiency

Your pricing can influence which PLG approaches could fit your business best. Let's say your ACV is above $30k, then you'll likely have some form of sales involved in your Go-to-Market. This can still be supported by PLG of course, however it's likely not only product-led.

At this deal size there are often different factors at play. Like multiple decision makers to manage, drafting up implementation plans or simply the desire of the customer to speak with someone. All these topics are well-suited for a sales rep to help with and at this contract value the economics of that can work out.

When we look at an ACV between $10k and $30k then that becomes harder, especially with the increased competition we see nowadays. Some form of Product-Led Onboarding can be beneficial in this case to provide the sales team with Product Qualified Leads for higher conversion. This is also where free trials or a freemium model can be worth considering. Through that the product can select good-fit customers from your audience.

For an ACV below $10k, an approach with a product-led focus is a must have nowadays, even if you have a sales team in place. The team will need to have conversion rates well above the usual inbound or outbound metrics and this is exactly what you can achieve with PLG.

Lastly, there's the Land and Expand approach. Even if your ACV is above $30k, you can offer a lower priced product-led offering. After the first deal, you can then sell the bigger contract as an expansion.

Reliance on customer-facing teams

We also need to assess how heavily your existing new business process relies on your sales and CS teams. It could be that your process is currently heavily people-driven. Meaning, for example, that a conversation with sales is required to buy and CS guides new customers through their onboarding. In that case introducing some form of Product-Led Onboarding can be a good area to start applying PLG. This will also be an enabler for many of the other PLG strategies. It will be hard to drive top of the funnel growth through PLG if there is no way to start using your product through self-service.

Even when introducing PLO, you can still decide to assign a CSM to high-value customers but at least the option of self-service onboarding exists and is used by a segment of your new customers. This will help with organizational efficiency and identifying good-fit customers.

PLO can be implemented in various ways. It can for example mean that new customers speak with sales first but then the rest of the onboarding is product-led or it can be a free trial that engages the user in the product before speaking with sales. Any combination should be possible as long as it drives the results you are aiming for.

A high reliance on sales and/or CS is also a good indication that there are possible efficiency gains from PLG. Imagine if you could get the same sales rep or CSM deal with twice the volume by leveraging the product. This would completely change the economics of your growth strategy. It can even allow you to serve customer segments or contract sizes that were previously not economically viable.

Flexibility of the pricing model

As a last step in the assessment, we look at the structure of your pricing model. We'll want to check if you have a set list price or if you always heavily discount your prices during sales conversations. In the latter scenario, it will be hard to build a self-serve buying process into your product.

If this is your situation then you could still look at Product-Led Onboarding and you can provide Product Qualified Leads (PQLs) for new business or for expansion. It will be hard though to automate the buying journey without a sales team involved because the quote for the customer cannot be standardized.

This is easier if your pricing can scale based on the number of users, certain product usage or if you have multiple products or add-ons that people can buy in addition to their initial contract. Then this provides a strong potential for Product-Led Expansion.

This could again enable a Land and Expand approach. You'll close the initial deal as fast as possible and then upsell. Even if the "land" part of this journey (i.e. customer acquisition) is not product-led, you could become product-led on the "expand" part. This can often be done with much less effort than what's required to drive top of the funnel.

Do the assessment

I've created a free online assessment to learn more about the situation your company is currently in. It's called the PLG Compass. For each of the PLG approaches, it will tell you how well positioned you are to start with it. It only takes a few minutes to fill out and you can save the results afterwards.

www.PLGandSales.com/compass

3. Driving the change

Now that we have an idea where to start, it's time to think about the execution and how we get buy-in from the organization. As with every organizational change, we will need to build a story to guide this journey and we will need to show results to validate that this initiative is driving the desired results.

Aligning key stakeholders

Before doing anything, you'll want to align with your key internal stakeholders on the goal for PLG. This will become your primary measurement of success.

If the goals you've been given are more general, such as: "we just want to grow" or "more revenue", then make sure to drill down and understand what exactly is meant. The implied goal might be more specific, such as entering a new market segment. Then it's important to be aware of this so you can come up with a targeted approach.

If no preference for the type of growth or revenue is given, then that gives you more options. It means you can look at new business revenue, expansion revenue, as well as reducing churn.

Start with quick wins

We can apply some of the best practices from change management, like starting with quick wins. Try to get to a first positive outcome with high confidence and low effort. This way you show the organization that investing in this area is a good thing. Even if revenue might not be coming in right away, there could be other metrics you can impact that will confirm that the path you are on drives results.

These quick wins can come in different forms. In some cases, it's a problem the organization has been having that you can solve through the product. Let's say you sell a product for which the ideal customer profile is in the United States but the sales team is getting demo requests from all over the world.

We can solve this through PLG. You could add an initial interaction in the demo request that will send the US companies straight to a meeting booking page and send other companies to an in-app experience that doesn't require sales. This should improve the booking rate for good-fit customers. It should also increase the conversion rates from the sales team. So it's a good starting point to get the organization onboard with further changes.

Now let's say you intend to add a self-serve edition of your product and currently people need to go through sales to get access. You'd want to show some early wins because this is typically a big project and investment. To test the demand for a product-led experience, you could add a signup button next to the demo request button on the website, even if you set the trial up manually. This will give you valuable insights into the impact of this approach on your Go-to-Market.

In a positive result, you would have more page conversions (i.e. leads) in total. Some people will book a demo and some will request a trial. Sales will receive higher quality leads and while the number of sales leads might have gone down a bit, revenue would remain roughly the same. This would be a great win for your product-led initiative. It would indicate that this approach brings in additional revenue.

It could of course also play out differently. Total conversions could stay the same and some of the good quality sales leads may prefer the product-led option. This would tell you to be more cautious as you build out this motion, as you are affecting existing revenue. It would also tell you though, that you have a customer segment that prefers the self-serve experience.

It could even be that nobody clicks the product-led option. That might mean it's better to put your focus elsewhere. More discovery would be recommended before building your onboarding experience to become self-service because your current audience doesn't seem to engage with it.

Set context on every update

As results come in, you'll want to share these with key stakeholders. Think of your executives or sales and marketing leadership. Remember that the frame of reference for people who are not familiar with PLG needs to be set on every update.

It doesn't matter if this is in a meeting or by email. Always start by reminding people what goals your project has set out to achieve and explain where you currently are on that journey. Only then elaborate on the most recent learnings.

In the last example, that means you would start with the intention to move to self-service onboarding because the company believes this will allow them to generate more revenue. As part of this, you explain the first experiment you designed and that you are testing this early on to increase the confidence in the chosen path.

Only after setting this context do you get to the results and even with the results it can be valuable to iterate that you are in a phase of experimentation; that you are trying to find the most effective growth path for the company. In that context, even a negative result is a valuable learning and should not be seen as failure.

If context is not set properly, here are some examples of things that could go wrong:

- People might have forgotten why the company is looking into this and who approved it.
- People might be unclear on the defined goal of the project.
- People might not understand how this will affect their role in the company (think of sales).
- People might not be familiar with growth experiments and how to interpret negative results.

In each of these cases, your message can be met with resistance or be misunderstood. So it's better to over-communicate on these things and assume that this frame of reference is not known when sending a message.

Dealing with objections

Even if you do all that, you might still run into objections from the sales team. This can signal that the context and goals of your product-led initiative are not understood.

The sales team knows how much revenue they can generate from the existing pipeline. Changes to the existing system endanger that revenue which, in turn, endangers the sales commission through which these teams are paid. So it's understandable that a new initiative like PLG raises concerns or objections and it's important to address them.

You need to be able to clearly explain the reasoning and business value of your product-led initiative. If you can't do that, then you haven't truly figured out what you are trying to do yet. You need to clearly communicate things like the business goal, the customer segment, and the intended approach, as well as how it plays together with the sales approach. If you do this well, then you should encounter much less resistance.

Data is your ally in these conversations. For example, try to show that you are capturing customers who don't engage with sales or that currently some customers are being oversold and churn more. That data will give you a business reason that all teams can get behind.

Align with existing growth initiatives

It's good to keep in mind that you should never be competing with the other Go-to-Market functions. There is only one growth that matters to the company, which is overall growth. Whichever way is the best way of achieving it, is how it should be done. Regardless of if you are in product, growth, marketing or sales.

PLG is not better than sales. It's just a different growth tactic. In some scenarios it indeed gets better results, in others it does not. Look at the result, not how it is achieved. You should always be operating as a team and never put your PLG initiative up against the existing growth motion. This will make people feel their jobs are at risk and it'll just result in resistance to your product-led initiatives.

To get people more warmed up, it's best to align your efforts with the existing direction of growth. Help the existing growth motions perform better, instead of creating your own independent version. Another way of aligning efforts is to clearly focus on another part of the market. For example focusing PLG on the SMB segment if the sales team is focused on mid-market and enterprise.

It's important to make this explicit. People's minds go to dark places when you let uncertainty drive their thoughts. So provide clarity and position the product-led efforts clearly. This will also enable others to promote the initiative because they can speak about it in the right context. You also enable them to provide further ideas on how this change could be realized.

You don't want to come across as a threat to the existing motion, especially while you are still collecting data and don't even know what is better. Down the road there can be scenarios where PLG will replace a part of the sales team's efforts but that doesn't happen overnight.

It also doesn't mean anybody needs to lose their job. Often it's more a question of refocusing on higher value work. Once you have the data, this is a much easier conversation to have. Until then, try to avoid confrontation and approach things with an open mind.

Evaluate progress together

I always like to discuss the progress with the revenue leadership. Take your time to set context and if necessary, educate them on how PLG works and why it can be beneficial to the business. Help them understand what the numbers mean, what they could mean for the business, and highlight how PLG could make their lives better and improve company results.

Try to be conscious that you are not operating in a vacuum. The sales organization is there and they have gotten the business to where it is today. Ignoring this would mean to ignore all the learnings that have been made over the past years. That doesn't mean that the company needs to keep doing what the sales team has been doing in the past years but the learnings are important input for your experiments, as well as for your communication with the sales organization.

Also, your work might affect people's jobs and sales leadership will have a say in how this gets implemented, so you want them to be informed and supportive. Not having a good understanding of the existing Go-to-Market can even make you look unknowledgeable because you don't understand the business.

Last but not least when you achieve a win in your PLG efforts, try to make it a joint win. Try to highlight the role of other stakeholders like sales and marketing. They will likely have helped in the preparation or execution of the initiative. Rarely do you do these things all by yourself and presenting it as a joint effort will increase your chances of creating positive momentum for PLG in the organization.

Interview with Franciska Dethlefsen

Amplitude

Introducing a self-service plan at Amplitude

"You can't just release the thing and expect that people will find it, use it, and pay for it. You have to educate them, make it visible, show what the feature is."

- FRANCISKA DETHLEFSEN

About Franciska Dethlefsen

Franciska is the Head of Growth Marketing at Amplitude where she's leading the charge on new user acquisition, activation & monetization. Prior to that, she was the Head of Growth at Iteratively, which was acquired by Amplitude. Before that, she built out the marketing function at Snowplow Analytics. All in all she has been doing growth for (product) analytics companies for the past 6 years, and also advises startups in the data and infrastructure space on their zero to one growth efforts.

Main takeaways

- A key concern was revenue forecasting and cannibalization of existing sales pipeline. This required extensive modeling to ensure the new plan provided additional value.
- Franciska explains how customer feedback drove the introduction of a new self-service plan. It also allowed

Amplitude to cater to a broader market segment with more accessible pricing.

- The plan also freed up sales resources to focus on higher-priced deals. The product would then handle lower-priced plans more efficiently.
- They were surprised that some customers upgrade to paid immediately upon signup. They also found that retention and churn needed attention, now that they serve monthly plans.
- Franciska stresses the importance of investing in feature awareness, user education, and continuous optimization. This is a requirement to make a product-led approach a success.

The full interview is available as a write-up, podcast, and video.
www.PLGandSales.com/interviews

Onwards

Standing the test of time

You now understand how PLG can be combined with your existing Go-to-Market operation and you have identified where you want to get started. This is where the actual work begins.

It can take time for results to come in. It can easily take 12 months to see the fruits of a new PLG acquisition approach. Other PLG approaches can be implemented faster but assume that it takes months to see results, not weeks.

There's a rule of thumb for timeline estimations in product development. You estimate how long you think something will take and then multiply that by three.

This is why you want to start with low effort experiments, to validate the approach you have in mind. Most experiments you run will fail and that's how you eventually learn what works. The speed at which you run experiments therefore correlates with the speed at which you grow.

Even a 12-month project can be divided into smaller steps with learning milestones. This will assure that what you release at the end of it, will have the desired impact. The trick is to stay calm and methodical. Lead with data in everything you do and put this data in the context of the company goals. This way you avoid opinions and keep the discussion on the facts.

With PLG you focus on developing user habits and delivering value. Even if revenue doesn't change immediately, this is how you build a good product, which should reflect in other metrics like customer satisfaction and retention. In the end, that's how you build a sustainable business.

Onwards!

THANK YOU!

After reading this book you understand the many ways in which you can combine PLG and sales to grow your business. In the years to come, PLG will be used by more and more companies to find new customers, increase Go-to-Market efficiency, and improve retention. Those that ignore this, risk being left behind.

If you found this book helpful, then I'd encourage you to share it with someone you know. Maybe a colleague or a friend who is trying to drive growth for their company.

To help others find this book, a review on Amazon would also go a long way. I would very much appreciate that, and I'm sure others would too.

Thanks for reading,
Vincent

WHAT'S NEXT

If you've read this far and you want more, subscribe to my free newsletter Growth Machines.

www.GrowthMachines.com

Beyond that, if you want help with your Product-Led Sales strategy, I can contribute in an advisory capacity.

If you'd like to learn more, send me an email at

vincent@PLGandSales.com

CREDITS

Written by

Vincent Jong

Interviews by

Ben Williams

Franciska Dethlefsen

Japna Sethi

Leah Tharin

Kyle Poyar

Pekka Koskinen

Todd Olson

Edited by

Ellen Fishbein

Jonathan Norman

Designed by

Leonardo Flores

Vanessa Mendozzi

Printed in Great Britain
by Amazon

57794940R00088